The Milk Industry in Uganda

Supply Chain and Liberalisation of the
Milk Industry in Uganda

Pamela Mbabazi

Fountain Publishers

Fountain Publishers
P. O. Box 488
Kampala
e-mail: fountain@starcom.co.ug
website: www.fountainpublishers.co.ug

ISBN 9970 02 494 9

Cataloguing-in-Publication Data

Mbabazi, Pamela
The Milk Industry in Uganda / Pamela Mbabazi.__ Kampala;
Fountain Publishers, 2005
__ p; __ cm.
Includes references maps, tables, charts and index

ISBN 9970-02-494-9
1. Milk processing – Uganda   2. Milk I. Title II. Author
637.149761

Table of Contents

Introduction

This book presents the results of an investigation into the redevelopment, redefinition and redirection of the milk industry in south-western Uganda. The study focused on small - and medium-scale milk production, processing and marketing in Ankole. The study assessed the impact of liberalisation on the milk industry in Uganda under President Yoweri Museveni's regime at the turn of the century, using the supply chains analysis framework as a methodological tool.

Although Ankole milk became plentiful after liberalisation, prices today are very low for the dairy farmers. Traders and processors have also faced immense challenges. During the rainy season, western Uganda produces approximately 60,000 litres of milk per day worth Ug. sh. 18 million, but much of it is not sold or processed. As a result approximately Ug. sh. 6.5 billion is lost annually.

The increase in the number of milk-processing plants in the wake of the liberalisation of the economy in the mid-1990s along with changes in technology, for example ultra heat treated milk (UHT), initially provided incentives for the revitalisation of the milk sub-sector. This generated employment and income opportunities not only for small - and medium-scale milk producers and processors in Ankole, but also for different people in milk-related enterprises elsewhere in the country. However, a multiplicity of problems has forced processing factories to close down.

The study further unveils the politics and economics of milk production and export, notably the impact of resource allocation on this milk industry by a variety of actors, including the state, civil society organisations and private companies. It analyses the structural, institutional and policy rigidities that continue to hinder the contribution of the milk industry to the development of Ankole. It is these bottlenecks that should be rectified if milk production is to promote human development in south-western Uganda.

Research for this study employed a range of techniques, including open-ended interviews with major stakeholders within the government and the private sector linked to the milk industry and local milk-producing and - exporting communities in Ankole and Kampala. Secondary sources, including the reports of concerned government ministries and institutions such as the Dairy Development Authority (DDA), the Uganda Investment Authority (UIA) and the export sector, were also consulted.

The analysis shows that the liberalisation of the Ugandan economy did initially lead to the rejuvenation and redevelopment of the milk industry in Ankole. Several milk factories were established in Mbarara and many small producers, vendors and processors benefited. Subsequently, however, the milk industry has faced a lot of seemingly insurmountable difficulties including: high input prices; insufficient demand for milk in and outside the country; inadequate capital; high taxes; the lack of regulation and unfavourable policies.

The main policy recommendation of this study is that, in order to enable milk, the key commodity in Ankole, to continue playing its vital role in the development of the region and the country at large, the government in partnership should deliberately promote the milk industry with none-state actors. The study proposes various scenarios to this effect.

1

Background of the Milk Industry in Uganda

The Milk Industry at Independence

Since the early colonial days, milk production in Uganda, has been concentrated in the western and south-western regions, particularly in the current districts of Mbarara, Bushenyi, Rukungiri, Kabale and Rakai. However, there were limited government efforts to develop a coherent and concerted policy for the milk sub-sector, after independence. The colonial and post-colonial governments gave greater assistance to crop farming than to the livestock sector. These governments were more interested in the cash crops export of which were earning the country substantial foreign exchange unlike the subsistence driven small scale milk production. For instance, the pastoral Basongora of Kasese District were driven out of their land to pave the way for the Bakonjo crop cultivators to grow cotton (Kisamba-Mugerwa, 1998).

In the 1960s, the first post colonial government placed more emphasis on commercial ranching through the Ankole-Masaka Ranching Scheme unproductive subsistence pastoralists gave away to progressive keep beef cattle farmers. Milk, therefore, was never an immediate pre-occupation at the time. Kisamba-Mugerwa (1998) argues that since the colonial days, state land tenure policies have aimed at the individualisation of land through the issuance of freehold and leased land titles to promote investment in land. Land in the pastoral areas was leased to individuals, co-operative societies and private companies to establish commercial ranches to produce beef for local consumption and export (Kisamba-Mugerwa, 1998). For this purpose, the Ankole- Masaka Ranching Scheme, an area that was previously occupied by the Bahima pastoralists up to 1920[1], was opened up in 1964 (Treadway, 1977). This in effect meant that the pastoral communities were driven out of their pastures. With the gazetting of Lake Mburo National Park into a protected area in 1982, shortage of grazing land become worse and the numbers of squatters increased tremendously from six families in 1985, to more than 100 families in 1992[2]. The government at the time felt that tourism would earn the country more foreign exchange than sub-dividing the land to accommodate more pastoralists and promote the livestock sector. This consequently hampered the growth and prosperity of the dairy industry in Ankole region.

A supply chain entails the full range of activities – inputs; outputs; technologies, communications, services, structural and governance structures – which are required to produce, market, distribute and deliver goods to the consumers. The final product in the hands of a consumer, therefore, results from the interplay of availability of the factors of production such as; the procurement of inputs, the laws and regulations in place (institutional framework), technology,advertising and marketing. Supply chains therefore link buyers and sellers of goods. According to Gary Gerrefi et al. (2001), business transactions, taking risks and bringing buyers and sellers together is done through the supply chains. Significant economies of scale exist in the supply chain processes involved in gathering products into economic lot sizes, processing and preserving them, packaging them into suitable units, finding buyers, selling transaction risk to third parties, providing credit to producers and moving products securely to ultimate consumers (Gerrefi et al, 2001). A supply chain of milk, therefore, is the flow of milk from the producer at the farm level, through the vendor or the milk processor to the wholesaler or retailer and finally, to the consumer. In the milk industry, all these activities have been undertaken by different actors under different circumstances during Uganda's history as is illustrated in next section.

The Milk Industry During Obote 1 Regime

During the Milton Obote I regime, the milk industry began to develop and clear and systematic supply chains began to form. Exotic breeds, as well as modern livestock farming practices like paddocking, proper animal care and spraying as well as disease control were gradually introduced. Exotic breed varieties mostly from Britain and Kenya paid for by the Overseas Development Agency (ODA) were air-freighted to Entebbe. The Obote I government was in the forefront of developing the milk industry. Dr John Babiha, the Vice-President and Minister of Animal Industry and Fisheries[3], a veterinary doctor, took the lead in the establishment of the dairy sector in Uganda during this period.

Trained veterinarians in the Ministry of Agriculture and Livestock helped to co-ordinate loans for the import of cows through local banks, imported and distributed accaricides at subsidised prices as well as subsidising the construction of dip tanks and fencing.

Organised milk collection and processing also began in the 1960s. Milk processing and distribution in Kampala was originally operated by a private company, the Uganda Milk Processing Limited, which imported fresh pasteurised milk from Kenya in green and yellow triangular tetra-packs. By an Act of Parliament, the Uganda Dairy Corporation (UDC) was established in 1967 as a government parastatal, with four main aims, namely: (i) to organise dairy farmers into dairy farmers' associations and co-operatives; (ii) to establish milk collecting centres and install coolers; (iii) to collect milk from the farmers and market it and (iv) to pay the farmers at the end of the month (Kasfir, 1994). Prior to this, there was no authority/organisations whether government or private, charged with the responsibility of promoting milk production in the country. So milk producers sold their milk individually to consumers mostly Asian businessmen and Europeans in towns.

With the establishment of the UDC, farmers began to sell their milk to the corporation, which enjoyed the monopoly of processing, packing and re-selling it countrywide. Until recently, no ultra-heat treated (UHT) milk was produced in Uganda. This shift in the milk industry from refrigerated bottles or tetra-packs of fresh milk to UHT boxes has tremendously extended the shelf life of the milk in the country. While all the milk processing technology during the Obote I period was imported, mostly from Britain, today the dairy industry relies on Swedish UHT technology and packaging materials from South Africa.

The supply chain for milk during the Obote I regime was very systematic and milk would flow from the producers often through co-operatives to UDC and then to consumers through retail shops mainly owned by Asians. Lesser amounts of raw milk flowed from the farmer, through the traders, to the consumer, see (Figure 1.1).

The Milton Obote I Government built dip tanks in different parts of Ankole and also provided inputs in the form of drugs, exotic breeds and other items. Farmers obtained these through the veterinary departments and co-operatives. Drugs as well as dip tank construction materials, poles and barbed wires were supplied at subsidised prices. Government supply shops where farmers could easily purchase farm inputs were opened in most parts of the country.

Figure 1.1: An expression of the supply chain for milk during the Milton Obote 1 regime

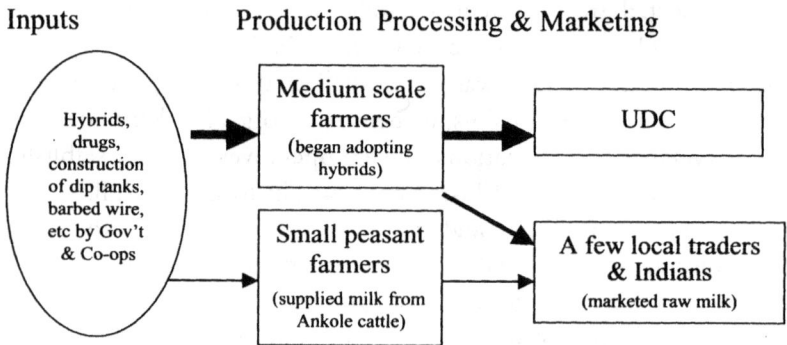

Inputs   Production Processing & Marketing

N.B: The thicker the line the heavier the supply flow.

Imported exotic dairy cattle gave greater milk yields than the indigenous breeds like the long horned Ankole cattle. However, to reduce dependence on imported breeds, government established breeding centres in different regions of the county. In Ankole, breeding centres were set-up at Nshara and Ruhengyere. The main aim of this was to multiply the herds and also to cross-breed the Ankole cattle in order to produce more milk and to provide farmers better quality breeds at affordable prices.

In addition, district farm institutes were established to serve as demonstration farms and to encourage farmers to adopt hybrid cattle. Workshops to educate farmers on best practices for livestock keeping and milk production were conducted in many parts of the country. For the first time, many Ugandans began to earn their living from just milk. Farmers were given loans and subsidies to establish dairy farms and many milk farmers' associations and co-operative societies were established around this period. In Ankole these associations included the Banyankore Growers Co-operative Union, the Bushenyi Dairy Farmers Association and the Rubaare Farmers Group[4]. However, milk productivity remained pretty low because the farm-gate price for milk was not attractive to farmers. Only the well-to-do were able to set-up dairy farms, but these were not numerous enough to satisfy the local demand. Besides, only the big dairy farmers could afford imported technology and to access state support in order to create profitable farms that produced milk on a sustainable basis (Kasfir, N: 1994). Most of the successful dairy farmers who adopted hybrids at the time were relatively wealthy. The poor farmers continued to depend on indigenous cattle for limited milk production and sale.

State action therefore played a central role in the development of the dairy in Uganda during the 1960s. Due to political instability that started in 1966 and the subsequent drop in demand for milk and its products, the dairy sector eventually collapsed, as did the entire economy. With the collapse of the dairy sector and the insufficient government effort to revive it, it is not surprising that by 1973, Uganda was still importing liquid milk from Kenya to satisfy the local demand.

The Milk Industry during the Idi Amin Period

The Idi Amin period was characterised by political instability and most of the government sectors declined. Amin expelled the Asian traders and later other foreigners and this greatly affected the economy, including the agricultural sector. His "Economic War" led to chaos in the operations of the economy. Agricultural input procurement became very difficult because foreigners refused to supply Uganda's imports on credit. Farmers lost the incentive to produce cash crops like coffee, tea and cotton, not only because official prices were too low, but also it took ages for farmers to be paid[5]. Interestingly, with inflation in the towns, the prices for milk and local foodstuffs rose sharply and during the mid-1970s it was more profitable to look after cattle than to grow coffee. As such more farmers in Ankole adopted cattle keeping and the sale of milk because their major source of livelihood[6].

However, during the Amin period, the state's capacity to serve dairy farmers shrank considerably and by 1977, milk collection from Ankole, for instance, rapidly declined from 10,000 litres in 1971, to less than 2,000 litres of milk in 1977. By 1979, the dairy corporation hardly collected any milk from Ankole (Kasfir, N: 1984). But diary farmers benefited from selling their milk to nearby urban centres and some areas like Bushenyi were able to sustain their production capacities (see section 2.2.1). Most farm inputs were bought through the black-market albeit at rather high prices to sustain their production.

Milk therefore, essentially flowed from the producers to the traders in nearby towns (see Figure 1.2). Except for traditionally processed products like cow-ghee and yoghurt, milk processing along the chain ground to a halt. UDC ended up also concentrating on marketing unprocessed milk, because it could not collect enough milk to sustain the processing capacity of its Kampala plant. Also, due to mismanagement and late or non-payment of farmers' milk, many farmers opted to supply to local traders instead of UDC. As such only a small fraction of the milk produced countrywide was marketed by UDC.

Figure 1.2: An Expression of the Supply Chain for Milk During the Idi Amin Regime

Inputs	Production	Processing (Non-Existant)	Marketing

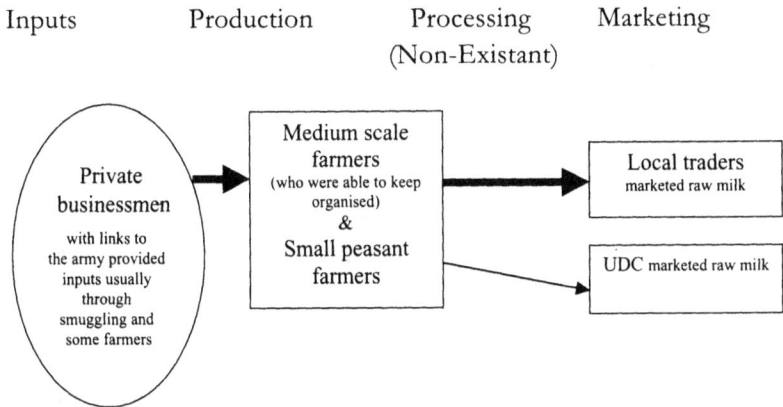

N.B: The thicker the line the heavier the supply flow.

The Milk Industry during the Milton Obote II Regime

The milk industry during the Obote II regime barely managed to limp on due to the prevailing civil disturbances. The Dairy Corporation plant in Kampala resumed its monopoly in buying, processing and marketing milk but continued to operate below capacity as transportation from upcountry was too expensive, risky and very unreliable.

At the farm level, the government made several attempts to revive the milk sub-sector by among other things, rehabilitating and promoting co-operatives, providing subsidies to farmers to rehabilitate their farms through the provision of credit and in some areas, initiating training programmes for farmers. Efforts were also made to renovate some district farm institutes, which in the 1960s had been used for demonstration to farmers. However, owing to political instability in much of the country, the achievements of these efforts were limited.

The continued collapse and disintegration of the economy and deterioration of the general political and social order affected the farmers dairy productivity nationwide. However, in some areas like Bushenyi, where farmers were more organised, alternative strategies were devised to purchase farm inputs, sustain their farms and market their milk[7].

In Nyakabirizi village near Bushenyi town, for instance, dairy farmers formed a communal dip association to run a dip tank built by the government in 1969. They were able to operate it effectively during the entire period of the Amin and Obote II regimes, when government subsidies were no longer forthcoming. Because investments in starting a dairy farm were quite substantial involving acquisition of imported breeds, drugs to keep them free from disease, which are also imported and continuous clearing of the farm, many farmers were determined to protect this investment. They strengthened their co-operatives to source for drugs, for instance, or marketed their milk by entering into contracts supply of milk to schools, hotels and other institutions within the region. According to Mr Mukaira, a prominent farmer-turned-educationist in Bushenyi since the early 1960s, when UDC became very inefficient, farmers in Bushenyi aggressively looked for new markets. Other farmers reduced their herds and brought smuggled drugs brought into the country by crafty businessmen with links to people in government[8].

Nelson Kasfir (1994) rightly argues that although farmers had came to expect state assistance for agricultural production and marketing, the guerrilla war in the early 1980s and the failure of the state to sustain its agricultural programmes farmers, were forced to form organisations and relied more on the market forces of supply and demand. Any observer who travelled in Bushenyi[9] during the 1980s was amazed to discover moderately large farms with pastures of 50 to 100 hectares, neatly divided into paddocks fenced with imported barbed wire and sustaining a herd of fifty or more imported pure breeds. Yet in other areas, farms were in a sorry state. Figure 1.3 shows the expression of a milk supply chain during the Obote II regime.

Figure 1.3: An Expression of the Supply Chain for Milk during the Milton OboteII Regime

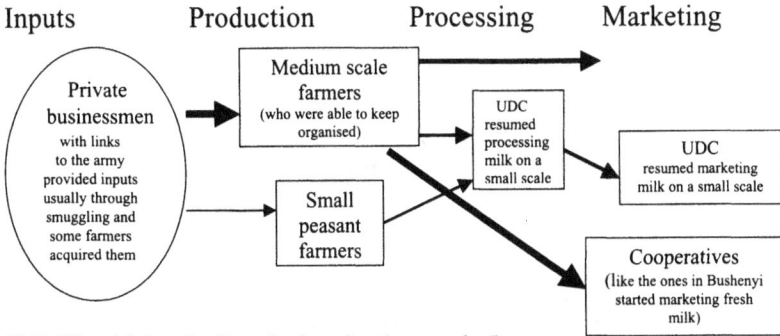

Inputs	Production	Processing	Marketing

Private businessmen
with links
to the army
provided inputs
usually through
smuggling and
some farmers
acquired them

Medium scale farmers
(who were able to keep organised)

Small peasant farmers

UDC resumed processing milk on a small scale

UDC resumed marketing milk on a small scale

Cooperatives
(like the ones in Bushenyi started marketing fresh milk)

N.B: The thicker the line the heavier the supply flow.

The Milk Industry during the Yoweri Museveni Regime

Under the National Resistance Movement (NRM) government of the Yoweri Museveni regime, particularly in the wake of liberalisation of the economy and the subsequent adoption of new UHT technology, the milk industry in Uganda was greatly rejuvenated. Today the dairy industry contributes six per cent of the national Gross Domestic Product (GDP), and milk consumption levels have increased from less than 20 litres, per person per annum, when the NRM took over, to 40 litres, per person, per annum, in 2001 (Land "O" Lakes, 2003). Still the milk industry faces a lot of challenges. A series of policy measures aimed at promoting the role of the private sector in the milk industry have been responsible for increased milk production during the Museveni period.

With the liberalisation of the economy, UDC's monopoly was dismantled and this led to the mushrooming of various milk cooling and processing factories countrywide. By 1994, six new milk processing plants had been established, four of which were located in Mbarara. The national cattle herd has also increased over the past fifteen years which in turn accounts for the livestock increased share of GDP.

By 1995, cattle dairy farming was reported to be on the increase, with most average farmers adopting "zero grazing"[10] and small-scale dairy farming. In 2001 the dairy herd nationwide was estimated at 158,883 exotics and crossbreeds compared to 140,000 five years earlier, which is a modest increase (UNCTAD/ICC, 2001). The most common types of exotic breeds in Uganda include; Friesian, Jersey, Guernsey, Ayrshire and Brown Swiss. The leading districts for exotic dairy farming in the country include Bushenyi, Mbarara, Ntungamo, Mpigi, Kabarole, Mukono, Kampala, Rukungiri, Jinja and Kabale (see Map 5).

In effect, therefore, it is during the Museveni era that milk production has increased tremendously. Some 520 million litres of milk were produced in 1995, while production in 2001 was estimated at 900 million litres. However, only about 10 percent of this, is processed. Other dairy products produced, albeit on a small scale, include UHT milk, butter, cheese, ice cream, yogurt and cow–ghee. Most of these products are consumed locally. The biggest market for milk in Uganda has always been Kampala. Export opportunities to neighbouring countries have not been given sufficient attention[11].

Map 1: Milk Producing Areas in Uganda

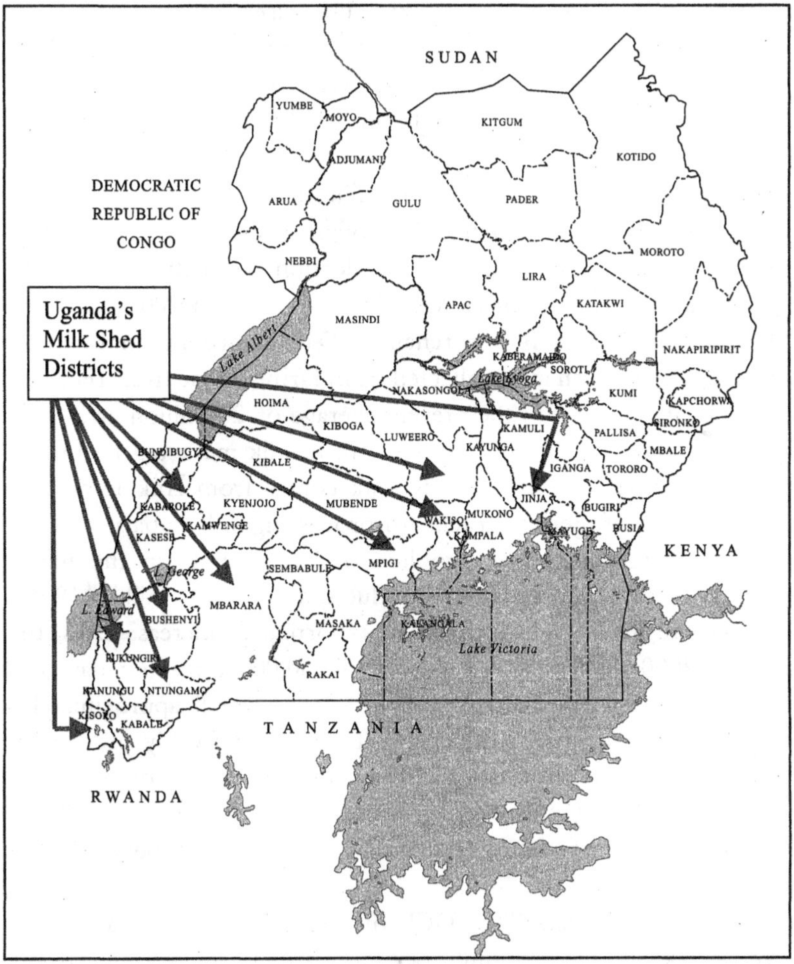

Specific policies adopted to boost the Milk Industry

One of the major policies that led to the boosting of the milk sector was the privatisation of public enterprises. Until 1992, when the government liberalised the milk sector, UDC was the only player in the formal milk market. It was, however, very incompetent and riddled with corruption. Due to mismanagement, its operations were very poor. It never collected or received milk on schedule.

Besides, its payment systems for the farmers' raw milk, was very inefficient. When the economy was liberalised, other processors joined the burgeoning milk sector to compete alongside UDC. This situation increased the demand for raw milk and served as an impetus to farmers to increase milk production nationwide especially in Ankole.

Alongside liberalisation of the milk industry, UDC was also restructured. It was rehabilitated through government and donor funding which raised the milk collection capacity from two operational collection centres in 1986 to over 60 in 2001 (*the New Vision* 21 July 2001). It was renamed Dairy Corporation Uganda Limited (DCL). Fresh milk collected from farmers rose from 186,000 litres annually in 1986 to the present average of 20 million litres per annum, accounting for 100 per cent fresh milk marketed by DCL. More than three quarters of this milk comes from Ankole and is transported in refrigerated trucks for processing in Kampala.

In order to reduce the problem of excess milk in the flush season[12], DCL ventured into the production of (UHT) milk in 1996. Furthermore, DCL went into active exporting to increase sales. In the year 2000, DCL co-packed of milk 30,000 litres per day for a Kenyan firm and a total of 248,963 litres worth approximately $78,000 were exported. In 2001, DCL exported freshly processed UHT milk to Kenya at an export level of 20,000 litres of milk per week. Unfortunately, this outlet was closed in the year 2002, largely because of political and market access disagreements between the two countries.

However, in March 2003, DCL officially re-launched its export drive of 300,000 litres of milk per month to Rwanda having been contracted by Laiterie de Nyabisindu, a Rwandan firm, to pack milk in the Viva Brand packs for the Rwandan market (*the New Vision* 21 July, 2003). DCL has also entered into a contract packing arrangement with Ola Dairies of Tanzania and hopes to expand its sales base as conditions get better. All these arrangements depict "new regionalisms" around the milk demand, packaging and supply in the liberalised era.

Liberalisation of the foreign exchange market also contributed to the expansion of the milk industry because it made access to foreign exchange easier and encouraged both foreign and domestic investors to invest in the dairy sector. The introduction of the Special Import Programme (SIP II) also impacted greatly on the milk sector. Milk processors were able to import machinery at subsidised tarrif rates and for the initial five year period, they were exempted from paying taxes as a way of promoting foreign investment in the sector.

Furthermore, as a result of the recommendations of the Dairy Master Plan study, the Dairy Industry Act (1998) was enacted leading to the creation of the (DDA), a body supposed to enforce hygienic milk processing and handling in line with the Public Health Act. The creation of investment bodies like (UIA) also greatly boosted the industry. The UIA gave assistance in the form of basic information and statistics to investors wishing to invest in any sector, including the milk sector, of the Uganda economy. Investors were helped to go through all bureaucratic procedures, like registration, fairly quickly. The aim was to make Uganda an attractive and competitive investment destination.

The return of Asian properties to their rightful owners also restored confidence among the Asian community, which has since played central role in the rejuvenation of the milk sector in general. For example, out of the four processing plants that were established in Mbarara following liberalisation, three were owned by Ugandan Asian returnees.

Other policies like the Plan for Modernisation of Agriculture (1997), the 'Animal Feeds Policy and Legal Framework (2001), the Veterinary Drugs Policy (2001), the Animal Breeding Policy Act (2001) and the Food and Nutrition Policy (2002) launched by government to alleviate poverty and modernise agriculture have also had a positive impact on the milk sector. Some farmers have been trained to improve the milk yields and earn more incomes. They have also been sensitised about how to improve their cattle feeds by growing grass supplements. In some areas like Nyabushozi and other dry semi-arid regions, the government has provided funds to construct valley dams and ensure easy access to watering points for farmers.

Other Initiatives to Boost the Milk Industry

Apart from government measures, donor agencies, including the Danish International Development Agency (DANIDA), the African Development Bank (ADB) and the Food and Agriculture Organisation (FAO) as well as Non-Governmental Organisations (NGOs) and other actors/partners in development have contributed to revitalise the milk industry in Uganda, especially before the era of liberalisation.

a) Donor Assistance

The rehabilitation of the milk industry was funded through loans and grants from several multilateral donor agencies, including the United Nations Development Programme (UNDP), the World Food Program (WFP), DANIDA and ADB. Related livestock projects were funded by the World Bank, the United States Agency for International Development (USAID), the European Economic Community (EEC) and other donors. By the end of 1992, up to $25.94 million out of a total external donor commitment of $55.1 million had been disbursed (see Table 1.1).

Table 1.1: Core projects of the rehabilitation of the dairy industry

Project	Donor	Duration	Disburse-ment (million $)	Type
Dairy rehabilitation	ADB	1987 – 1993	6.0	Loan
Dairy rehabilitation	DANIDA	1988 – 1993	5.2	Grant
Support to dairy industry	WFP	1989 – 1993	9.7	Grant
Dairy industry development	UNDP/ FAO	1987 – 1992	5.04	Grant
			Total: 25.94	

Source: FAO, 1992.

World Food Programme (WFP).

The WFP funding was providing assistance in the form of dried, skimmed milk and butter oil. These were recombined by the UDC to cover the shortfall in fresh milk supply during the dry seasons, in order to meet demand. The funding was also used to generate counterpart funds used to promote dairy development through, among others, support of dairy extension and farmer training; importation of farm inputs for sale to farmers; purchase of milk collection vehicles, and construction of milk-collecting centres for the UDC; the renovation of the Entebbe Dairy Training School buildings; and the maintenance of a small DDA secretariat in Kampala.

Danish International Development Agency (DANIDA).

DANIDA's main contribution was the rehabilitation of the UDC's main processing plant in Kampala and the upgrading of milk collection facilities in Mbarara. DANIDA also provided funds for equipment and machinery used to rehabilitate the Entebbe Dairy Training School and plant. The agency also financed a dairy sector study – the Dairy Master Plan Study – from which most of the plans to revive the industry were drawn.

The African Development Bank (ADB).

By 1992, loans extended by ADB to the Ugandan Government had been partly utilised to procure insulated road tankers, refrigerated milk distribution trucks, coolers and laboratory equipment for the UDC. Some of these loans were also used to restock and improve the infrastructure on government farms.

United Nations Development Programme/Food & Agriculture Organization (UNDP/FAO).

UNDP funding was used to support an FAO-executed technical assistance project - the Dairy Industry Development Project - whose purpose was to co-ordinate and implement an overall programme for dairy development in partnership with the Ministry of Agriculture, Animal Industry and Fisheries (MAAIF), the Dairy Corporation, the DDA and farmers' groups. FAO fielded and funded several international and national dairy specialists/consultants in development, management, accounting, technology, engineering, production, veterinary science, extension, training and marketing.

b) NGOs and the Re-Development of the Milk Industry

Following the liberalisation of the Ugandan economy, many NGOs, both local and foreign, emerged and started to offer their services in the milk sector. They include Land O'Lakes, the Heifer Project International and the South-western Uganda Milk Producers Co-operative Association (SUMPCA), to mention but a few. Other NGOs like Send a Cow and various churches have also been involved in promoting the dairy industry in Ankole and nationwide. Table 3.3 gives a glimpse at their main areas of focus.

Table 1.2: NGO Support for the Milk Industry

Name	Since	Area of Support
Land O Lakes	1991	• Training of farmers & assisting them to improve milk quality • Assisting farmers to form cooperatives • Assisting processors to get market • Increasing awareness among the population about the need to drink good quality milk
Heifer Project International	1982	• Distributing in-calf heifers (see page 184) • Training farmers • Providing soft loans to farmers
Send a Cow	1988	• Providing semen • Providing in-calf heifers
SUMPCO	1998	• Training of farmers
The Church of Uganda Livestock Improvement Project	1983	• Providing in-calf heifers
Uganda Catholic Secretariat Dairy Project	1987	• Providing in-calf heifers

Source: Author's Fieldwork, 2003

Land O' Lakes Inc. is an International NGO aimed at promoting the livestock (particularly the dairy) industry worldwide. It began its operations in Uganda in the early 1990s and has been instrumental in promoting the dairy sector by carrying out such activities like, organising the June Dairy Month (JDM) activities to increase awareness among the population on the benefits of drinking milk, though these are still on a small scale. Land O' Lakes is also involved in sensitising farmers about better methods of keeping animals. In partnership with USAID, it has assisted dairy farmers, producers and their cooperatives and associations to develop their businesses in order to create opportunities for the growth of the dairy industry (The New Vision 15 June 2000). Furthermore, together with DDA, Land O' Lakes has organised and encouraged farmers to form cooperatives to improve milk marketing. Land O' Lakes, in conjunction with the National Bureau of Standards, has also initiated collaboration with the milk vendors to formulate a draft code of practice for handling and marketing raw milk. Other agencies like the USAID-funded 'Support for Private Enterprise Expansion and Development' (SPEED) have also been increasingly co-operating with Land O" Lakes and the Heifer Project International to improve the dairy industry.

The Heifer Project International is another international NGO that provides exotic breeds to farmers free of charge in an effort to promote people's incomes. It mainly focuses on the low income households and in particular the women who need an extra source of income to support their families. As a result, many households have engaged in zero-grazing with the support of this NGO and are now producing milk which has become their main source of income.

South-western Uganda Milk Producers Co-operative Association is another NGO that has given support to the dairy industry in Uganda. SUMPCA owes its origins to the research findings of Mbarara French Milk Project, a consultancy project commissioned by government to investigate the problems of the milk sector in Mbarara District. This research found it imperative to bring farmers under one umbrella for them to benefit from milk production and to have a uniform voice in pursuing their interests. SUMPCA was thus formed around 1998, with the assistance of two French experts.

Currently, sponsored by the French Embassy in Uganda, SUMPCA operates in the districts of Mbarara and Kabale and started with 22 farmers selected from a total number of 184 farmers originally sampled. SUMPCA has a membership of approximately 59 farmers. Its overall objective is to organise and educate farmers to supply better quality and hyeginic milk products. This NGO has among other things, carried out on-farm demonstration activities with its pioneer members, arranged field trips for farmers to Kenya for educational purposes and sensitised farmers on improved methods of milk production, handling and marketing. SUMPCA works closely with other agencies like DDA, Land O' Lakes and (UNIFA). However, illiteracy, poor logistical support and lack of co-operation from some farmers has limited the expansion of SUMPCA's activities in much of Ankole.

In conclusion, it is important to note that the supply chains for the milk industry have been changing since independence. Table 3.4 presents a summarised version of the chronology of types of milk supply chains from the Obote 1 regime in the 1960s to Museveni's era at the beginning of the twenty first century.

Table 1.3: Chronology of Types of Milk Supply Chains & Changing Governance Structures

	Changing Milk Chains & Governance Structures
Milton Obote I Regime	• Government initially promotes the dairy sector • Fairly systematic supply chain with government exercising full power in ensuring the supply of quality milk • Farmers' co-operatives and other government ministries and parastatals quite strong and able to regulate operations of the sub-sector and ensure quality • Only fresh & pasteurised milk sold • Not enough/sufficient milk produced locally • Only UDC a government parastatal processing and marketing milk

Idi Amin Regime	• Break down of state apparatus and hence no apparent / very problematic milk supply chains, generally • In areas where farmers were able to maintain co-operatives, local refined supply chains of milk sustained; e.g., in Bushenyi • Only fresh milk sold • Not enough/sufficient milk produced locally • No regulatory mechanisms and the army pretty much in control...., especially of the lucrative agricultural supply chains for such export commodities like coffee
Milton Obote II Regime	• Systematic supply chains for milk being revived particularly with the revival of co-operatives and rehabilitation of the government parastatal, UDC • Increased insecurity prevented further progress of the milk & livestock sub-sectors • Only fresh and pasteurised milk sold • Only UDC, a government parastatal, processing and marketing milk • Not enough/sufficient milk produced locally
Yoweri Museveni regime	• Clear supply chains for milk begin to form initially with liberalisation, especially with the rehabilitation of DCL and entrance of many more actors. • Sufficient milk produced locally and some exported initially • UHT milk processed and sold by both DCL and private processors • The lack of regulation on the part of government, however, meant that the milk supply chains to-date especially in Ankole have become very problematic with the emergence of the informal milk supply chain (see chapters 4 & 5) • More NGO involvement in the milk sub-sector

As Table 1.3 shows, the milk industry in the mid-1990s was greatly rejuvenated with the liberalisation of the economy and several actors namely the government, civil society and private companies have all been involved in its revitalisation. Additionally, policies undertaken by the NRM government had a positive impact (at least initially) on the milk industry as was illustrated by the increases in milk yields. The performance of the milk industry is nonetheless volatile and this dissertation suggests that the many constraints in the milk supply chain (which will be discussed in subsequent chapters) have hindered the development of the milk sub-sector. Hence this study analyses the challenges and opportunities of the milk industry and addresses what needs to be done to promote its role in advancing human development in Ankole. The next chapter presents a summary of the major findings from the analysis of the contemporary milk supply chain in Ankole.

2

The Milk Industry in Ankole

Ankole, a predominantly cattle keeping region is the largest region of milk production in the country. A large percentage of the population (60 per cent) depends on the sale of livestock and livestock products as a source of livelihood. It is mainly the small farmers grazing indigenous cattle and crossbreeds on fenced and at times, unfenced communal lands, who produce much of the milk. These account for approximately more than 70 per cent of the milk produced in the region (Land O' Lakes 2001). Other milk producers include medium-scale commercial dairy farmers who graze their crossbreed and exotic cattle on individual perimeter fenced land-holdings and zero-grazers of exotic cattle.

A Description of the Study Area

This research concentrated on the south-western part of Uganda comprising present day Mbarara, Bushenyi and Ntungamo districts, which is known as Ankole region. It is largely inhabited by the Banyankore, comprising of the Bairu being the majority ethnic group and the Bahima, the minority. Traditionally, the latter used to be the cattle keepers and the Bairu were the cultivators, but nowadays both groups have taken up cattle keeping and in particular dairy farming as a means of livelihood.

Ankole region is surrounded to the east by the grasslands of Rakai District and to the west by Lake Edward and Rukungiri and Kabale districts. In the south, it is separated from Tanzania by the Kagera River, while to the north and north-west is a chain of water bodies forming Lake George extending through to Kazinga Channel and linking back to the Lake Edward. (see Map 1)

Ankole forms part of the 'cattle corridor' leading from the grasslands of the upper Nile up to the plateau of Rwanda and

Tanzania. This corridor is typical of the African Savanna with its rolling, grass-covered hills and sparse acacia scrub. It is an area of great natural beauty (Bamunoba Y.K, 1973).

Map 2: The Ankole Region

Source: Uganda's Districts Information Handbook 2002

The three districts, which form Ankole region (i.e. Mbarara, Bushenyi and Ntungamo) have a total landmass of approximately 15,231 sq. km, with Mbarara being the largest at approximately 10,154 sq km, followed by Bushenyi which is approximately 4,026 sq. km and lastly, Ntungamo (see Map 4) which has a land mass of approximately 1,051 sq. km[13].

According to the 2002 National Census, the population of Mbarara district was 1,089,051; Bushenyi 723,427 and Ntungamo 386,815, giving a total population of 2,199,293 people[14]. In terms of population density, however, Bushenyi has the highest at 189 followed by Ntungamo at 118 and, lastly, Mbarara at 113. Variations in the population density have greatly determined the type of livestock production systems adopted in each of the districts and consequently, influenced the levels of milk production in each.

By most developmental parameters, the rather young district of Ntungamo compares less favourably with Mbarara and Bushenyi districts. With a few exceptions, the entire region has rich agricultural lands and receives heavy and evenly distributed rainfall during most months of the year, except for the pastoral corridor of Kashari and Nyabushozi.

Generally, Ankole region lies at an altitude of between 129m – 1,524m above sea level with temperatures averaging between 25 – 27⁰c. The rainfall is medium reaching up to 1,200 mm, per annum, in some areas. There are two significant wet seasons: September to November and March to April. During these months, the milk producers have considerably higher outputs in terms of milk supply. During the dry seasons, however, the pasture and water for cows greatly declines[15].

The Development of the Milk Industry in Ankole

Although there are plenty of oral stories, newspaper reports and unsorted records regarding the development of the milk industry in Ankole, no attempt has been made to study and evaluate the history and political economy of this very crucial sector in Ankole region. Furthermore, not much has been researched or written to explain the impact of liberalisation on this sector today by examining the changing supply chains around the milk industry. Yet, it is the source of livelihood for the majority of peasants, traders and various people in the region. My thesis sought to rectify such neglect.

The Introduction of Exotic Cattle Breeds in Ankole

In order to understand the processes around the supply chain organisation of milk in Ankole today and what impact liberalisation has had on this sub-sector, it is necessary to explain the factors behind the increase of milk production in Ankole since the adoption of hybrid cattle, which currently account for a considerable portion of the milk produced in this region.

At the time of independence in 1962, most cattle keepers in Ankole owned the Ankole long horned breed. Most of these cattle keepers were the Bahima who grazed their cattle on unfenced perimeter land in the areas of Kashari, Ntungamo and Nyabushozi. Although cattle-keeping was traditionally a speciality of the Bahima ever since the pre-colonial period, by the beginning of the 1970s, the Bairu owned two thirds of cattle in Ankole, mostly the hybrids (Kasfir, Nelson: 1994). The Uganda government, under Milton Obote I, introduced exotic animals from Kenya and UK to improve milk production. These animals gave high yields per cow (up to 30 litres of milk per day), compared to the average Ankole cow that produced only 1 litre of milk per day. Experimental stations were opened in several places including Nshara government ranch and Ruhengyere Experimental Station, both in Ankole, for cross-breeding purposes.

Local farmers were encouraged to form co-operatives in order to get technical assistance in establishing farms. Exotic animals were sold to local farmers at subsidised prices through the veterinary department. This was direct support from the government under the Ministry of Animal Husbandry, Game and Fisheries. Other forms of assistance given to farmers included the building of dip tanks, the clearing, fencing and paddocking of farms, the providing of seeds for improved grass varieties, on-farm training by extension workers, the providing of subsidised drugs and accaricides as well as loans for the purchase of various other inputs.

According to Mr Mukaira, a prominent farmer turned educationist from Igara in Bushenyi District, too many farmers are now dependent on milk as their main source of income. The government needs to design or adopt a deliberate policy to revive this sector.

As he put it, "The future is bleak for the milk industry in Uganda today unless something is done."[16] Mr Mukaira was one of the first farmers in Ankole to start the keeping of exotic breeds cattle for milk production, prior to the establishment of the breeding centres in Ankole in 1963. He indicated that adopting hybrid cattle for milk production was largely due to government support resulting in his relative success.

He stressed that livestock keeping is a tiring job. Milking cows demands the full and continuous attention of a farmer, yet most cattle keepers in Ankole tend to be part-time farmers. This, he asserted, was one main reason for the poor performance of this sector.

Mr Mukaira says he acquired his first exotic cattle when he was encouraged by an agriculturalist to venture into exotic cattle to supplement to his low teacher's salary, Mukaira bought the first two in calf friesian cows from Delmira Dairy Farm in Kenya with a loan of E. A. shillings 2,000/= from bank, which, at the time, had three conditions for accessing loans, namely, a title deed, a current account with the bank and life insurance. He struggled to meet these conditions by saving his salary for quite a long time and was eventually given the green light. He bought the two in-calf cows at E. A. shillings 1,050/= and 950/= respectively. Unfortunately, one of the cows died in transit, but the surviving one produced a calf. This yielded 20 litres of milk, per day. Mr Mukaira pointed out that the change in environment affected the health of the lactating cow and it also died after 4 months, partly because his farm management skills at the time were poor. Despite these setbacks, he never lost faith and decided to try again by investing in farm improvement first. On the advice of the veterinary department he double fenced his farm and cleared a strip of grass all around it which had to be swept regularly in order to prevent the intrusion of ticks.

On his second attempt, Mr Mukaira teamed up with three other farmers. This time all the cattle survived. A lot of milk started to be produced in Bushenyi and most of this was sold to the Asian community in town, which at the time was quite substantial. Gradually, as the number of farmers increased, a cooperative was formed (Bushenyi Dairy Farmers' Association), which finally won a tender to supply milk to the Uganda Transport Company (UTC) a parastatal. Within three years Mr Mukaira had multiplied his cattle and was selling them to other farmers. Following Mukaira's example with the market for milk assured, more and more farmers in Bushenyi started keeping exotic breeds. The government's deliberate policy to support and encourage farmers to keep exotic and cross breeds inspired the development of the milk industry in other parts of Ankole. However, as Mr Mukaira interestingly noted, it took quite some time for the locals in Bushenyi to take to drinking milk from the hybrids. He explained that, in the first few months, the locals refused to buy his and other farmers' milk from the exotic cows claiming it smelt bad. But with the intensification of government's sensitisation programmes at the time, people's perceptions and consumption habits began to change.

Mr Mukaira further noted that in 1970, the government constructed a dip-tank for him at a subsidised rate. The government also purchased a milk cooler for the co-operative society and according to him, this was done elsewhere in Ankole in support of farmers who where keeping pure breeds. During this time, the milk industry in Ankole was at its height because the government was providing subsidies like constructing dams for farmers at 40% subsidy, providing grass species for improved pastures and barbed wire, poles and drugs at subsidised rates.

Mr Mukaira's pioneering experience was shared by approximately over 100 farmers throughout Ankole who had access to government assistance at the time. Gradually, the number of farmers who adopted exotic breeds increased in many parts of Ankole, often with government assistance. According to Dr Berinde, however, it is mostly in Bushenyi that farmers got high yielding breeds largely because the temperatures are cooler and the population more receptive to change, as opposed to the more conservative Banyankore from other parts of Ankole, particularly Nyabushozi, Kazo and Rushenyi Counties[17].

3

The Impact of Liberalisation

Major Findings

With the advent of liberalisation in Uganda, the sale of milk increasingly became a key revenue generating activity for producers, particularly in the districts of Mbarara, Bushenyi and Ntungamo. Many investors joined this sub-sector and several factories were set up, leading to an increase in milk farm gate prices (NEMA: 1999) and a rise in incomes among a large cross-section of milk producers throughout south western Uganda. The dismantling of the Uganda Dairy Corporation (UDC), which was a quasi-monopoly, gave way to the setting up of a number of milk cooling and processing plants. In Mbarara alone, an area commonly referred to as "always flowing with milk and honey," more than five milk-processing factories sprung up. The establishment of privately-owned milk plants following the liberalisation of the industry undoubtedly gave impetus to small and medium scale farmers to increase milk productivity in Ankole. According to NEMA (1999), milk production in south western Uganda increased from 35,000 litres in 1987 to 450 million litres in 1996 and to 670 million litres in 1999. In a recent radio statement, Hon. Mary Mugyenyi, the State Minister for Animal Husbandry, stated that there has been a tremendous increase in annual milk production nationwide, approximately one billion litres,(more than half of which comes from Ankole) and that the government was making plans to export the excess milk to other countries (CBS News: **www.cbsfmbuganda.com/news**).

However, over the recent past, the milk processing industry has been confronted with a number of problems[18]. Although initially, Ankole milk was exported to Kenya, Tanzania, the Democratic Republic of Congo (DRC) and even Southern Sudan, by the year 2000, because of various restrictions imposed by some of these countries and numerous supply constraints, some of the factories had gradually collapsed. The liberalised era, therefore, has witnessed the rise and fall of ultra-heat treated (UHT) milk-processing industries in Mbarara (see section 3.6.5). To-date, most of the factories have closed down but milk continues to be plentiful, hence the prices of raw milk are very low, leaving many farmers frustrated.

The milk industry has faced numerous challenges in production and marketing, as well as in the management/governance spheres following liberalisation of the economy. In the first place, government policy for the promotion of the milk industry has not been clear and in some cases, is contradictory. In terms of marketing, the policy guidelines relating to quality assurance are not well implemented and this has in effect resulted in the milk vendors marketing sub-standard milk, which is severely adulterated and contaminated, to the detriment of the industry and the health of population. Furthermore, all the processing machines and UHT packaging materials utilised in this industry are acquired from abroad and government has not made any effort to assist the industry in building its technical capacity. So all the milk processors rely on foreign experts to maintain these machines in addition to importing expensive packaging methods and spares. The lack of technical support therefore poses a problem to the milk processing industry.

Another impact of liberalisation has been the state's shrinking capacity to provide continuous support services to dairy farmers. As a result, farmers all over the country have not been cushioned against market forces, especially in connection with imported farm inputs. The collapse of co-operatives, which in the past used to serve as channels for the state to provide support services to farmers in the form of production implements and marketing, has made the situation worse because the prices of imported farm inputs have sharply risen during the era of liberalisation. This has in most cases resulted in higher production and marketing costs[19]. At the moment, milk producers are not getting enough inputs and also lack sufficient access to extension workers. As a result, it is now common to find a cow which would normally produce 30 litres a day, now producing a mere five litres a day because of poor feeding, poor milking and general lack of awareness on the part of the farmer on how to increase milk yields. Nevertheless, milk in this region remains plentiful although the incomes and the growth and expansion of the milk industry is greatly depressed.

The Current Milk Supply Chain

From the study, it was found that both the informal and formal milk chain supply exists in Ankole. The relationship and co-ordination of key actors in the current milk supply chain in Ankole is shown in Figure 3.1.

Figure 3.1: An Illustration of the Key actors & their Relationship in the Current Milk Supply Chain in Ankole

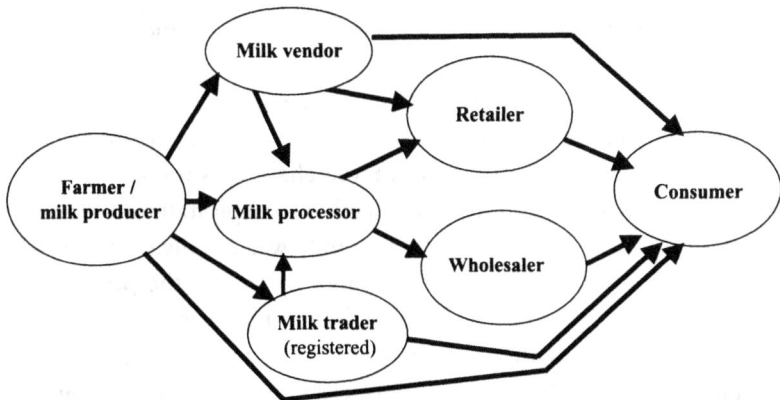

The milk supply chain in Ankole today evidently starts with a village milk producer. He or she owns the land and cattle and produces milk for sale and home consumption. The farmer either sells his/her milk in its raw form directly to the consumer or to the milk vendor, the milk trader or the milk processor. The vendor either sells the fresh milk directly to the consumer, or to the retailer or even to the milk processor, especially during the dry season when fresh milk is in short supply. The licensed milk trader, can also sell the milk to the consumer or milk processor. Milk traders in Ankole usually transport the raw milk to the Kampala market where there is a big demand for Ankole milk. The milk processor processes and packs the milk after which he/she sells the milk to a retailer or wholesaler who in turn gets the milk to the customer.

The volume of milk handled within the supply chain where the producer sells milk directly to the consumer is the smallest and the price in this chain is the lowest, often not more than Ug sh 50 a litre. The producer sells larger milk quantities to the vendor, who in turn sells it to the customer. Here prices may range between 50 and Ug sh 100 on average. The milk handled through traders in the chain is also considerably high and in this case the average prize is Ug sh 150. The processors often offer a higher price of approximately Ug sh 200 per litre.

The complex supply or delivery of milk from the farmer to the consumer has its pros and cons. The process is handicapped by certain constraints that have been compounded by liberalisation. There are many problems facing the farmer, the vendor, the milk trader and the processor, before the milk gets to the consumer. The producer who is at the lowest end of the chain gets the lowest price and has become more and more vulnerable to exploitation in this era of liberalisation. Prior to liberalisation, milk was usually sold through co-operatives but UDC monopolised the buying and the processing. To some extent, farmers had a voice, but today, much of the trade carried out directly with the farmers, which puts them in a weaker bargaining position. In Bushenyi, farmers are reviving co-operatives and getting more involved in milk marketing in order to influence prices. Nevertheless, the over-supply of milk nowadays and the fall in prices, has left Ankole farmers at the mercy of the vendors, traders and the processors who dictate the farm gate prices. The farmers' loss of bargaining power has become a source of frustration and posses a threat to the long-term development of the milk sub-sector.

As already mentioned, the milk supply chain in Ankole entails, the flow of milk from the farm level, through the traders and vendors as well as processors and finally to the consumer. This process takes two forms; the more organised or "formal" supply chain for processed milk and the more "informal" chain for unprocessed milk, which appears to be more problematic due to the continuous entry and exit of different agents from time to time, particularly in this era of liberalisation. It is important to note that of the total amount of milk produced in Uganda, more than 80 per cent is consumed without being processed which means that the supply chain for unprocessed milk is more voluminous and gives the vendors and licensed milk traders the lion's share of the milk trade in Ankole and indeed the country.

Figure 3.2 shows the unprocessed and the processed supply milk chain in Ankole. Evidently, in the processed milk chain, raw milk is sold to processors who in turn supplies processed milk to the consumer, mainly through supermarkets, retailers, and agents throughout the country. Figure 3.2 shows that pastures, drugs, and veterinary care are the main inputs at the farm level. At the processing level, taxes, machinery, labour, working capital and management are the main processing inputs in the supply chain (see Figure 3.2).

Figure 3.2: A Detailed Expression of the Milk Supply Chain in Ankole for Unprocessed & Processed Milk

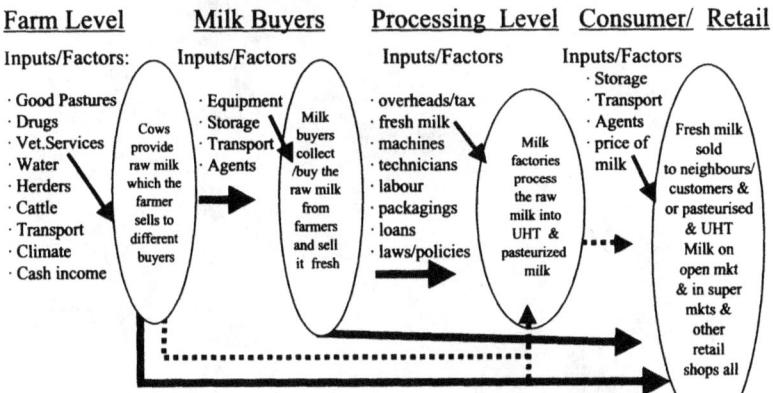

Farm Level	Milk Buyers	Processing Level	Consumer/ Retail
Inputs/Factors:	Inputs/Factors	Inputs/Factors	Inputs/Factors
· Good Pastures · Drugs · Vet.Services · Water · Herders · Cattle · Transport · Climate · Cash income	Cows provide raw milk which the farmer sells to different buyers	· Equipment · Storage · Transport · Agents — Milk buyers collect /buy the raw milk from farmers and sell it fresh	· overheads/tax · fresh milk · machines · technicians · labour · packagings · loans · laws/policies — Milk factories process the raw milk into UHT & pasteurized milk	· Storage · Transport · Agents · price of milk — Fresh milk sold to neighbours/ customers & or pasteurised & UHT Milk on open mkt & in super mkts & other retail shops all

Source: Author's Fieldwork Jan-May 2003

N.B: The thicker straight lines depict the heavier flow of raw unprocessed milk in the informal milk chain while the dotted lines depict the flow of milk in the formal milk chains, which are regulated and more organised.

An examination of the unprocessed milk chain shows that milk from the farm level is sold to vendors who either sell this milk to customers as raw milk, or to the processors, especially during the dry season when fresh milk is in short supply. Also, licensed milk traders who buy cheap raw milk from farmers in Ankole, usually through agents and transport the raw milk to Kampala for sale. Other towns along the Mbarara-Kampala route also offer alternative milk outlets albeit on a smaller scale.

Primary milk production in Ankole is mainly done by small-scale rural households who own on average between 10 to 20 cattle. From a sample of 105 farms visited during the research for this study, it was established that the majority of farmers in the region still own the indigenous long-horn cattle breed (see Figure 3.3). Cross breeds and exotic cattle account for less than 20 per cent of the total cattle population in Ankole (See Table 4.2). Nevertheless, the adoption of hybrids has increased since the time they were introduced in the early 1960s and major changes have taken place since the liberalisation of milk processing and marketing in Ankole.

Figure 3.3   Long-horned Ankole Cattle

The major dairy production system in Ankole is the grazing of indigenous and improved breeds on individual parameter fenced landholdings. However, grazing indigenous cattle on unfenced communal pastures is also still common as shown in Figure 3.3. Several farmers in the region, particularly in Bushenyi District, have now adopted to keeping exclusively hybrid cattle in perimeter fencing and have established fairly modern farms (see Figure 4.4). These produce considerable volumes of milk - on average 100 litres of milk per day for each farm.

Figure 3.4 High-Breed Cattle in Ankole

From the field research, it was established that farmers in Igara and Sheema counties in Bushenyi District the proportion of cross-breeds to local breeds is higher than in Mbarara and Ntungamo districts (see Table 3.1). Of the 15 farmers visited in Igara county, for instance, none owned local breeds whereas in Sheema only three farmers owned local breeds alongside the hybrids. This is largely due to the conducive cool climate and evergreen pastures as well as the willingness of the local community to adapt to change and to embrace new ideas.

Table 3.1: Milk Production Levels for Selected Farmers in Different areas of Ankole

Area	Number of farmers interviewed	Total number of cows owned by selected farmers	Total number of local breeds	Total number of cross & high breeds	Total milk prod. (litres)	Highest milker (litres)	Lowest milker (litres)
Nyabushozi	15	3,330	2,032	1,178	2,624	15	1
Kashari	15	1,840	155	1,615	2,892	20	2
Isingiro	15	1,262	633	628	760	14	1
Igara	15	669	-	515	2,490	25	3
Sheema	15	563	48	669	1,254	32	4
Rubaare	15	769	462	307	496	12	1
Ruhaama	15	990	532	458	612	10	1
TOTALS	105	9,423	3,862	5,370	11,128	-	-

Source: Author's Fieldwork, March 2003

Milk production in Ankole is very seasonal and highly dispersed geographically. This is because livestock productivity and milk production in particular, have always depended on natural pastures and the use of rudimentary technologies. Most producers own approximately 20 to 30 head of cattle, grazing on approximately 1 to 2 acres of land and producing on average 30 litres of milk per day. In Nyabushozi farmers own Ankole cattle in large numbers (sometimes over 2000) and hold up to 100 acres.

The largest milk producing areas within Ankole have always been Kashari, Nyabushozi, Kazo, Rubaare, Ruhaama, Sheema and Igara. Increases in milk production since liberalisation vary from district to district. According to the annual milk production estimates by DDA for the years 1992 and 2001, Bushenyi, for instance, produced approximately 43 million litres and 99 million litres respectively, while Ntungamo district produced 25 million litres and 37 million litres respectively. It is Mbarara District that achieved the highest increases in milk production in the whole country from approximately 92 million litres in 1992 to 200 million litres in 2001. This confirms that this milk-shed[20] region has enormous potential not only to produce milk and milk products for domestic consumption but also for export if only the existing challenges can be addressed.

Milk production on farms in Ankole is influenced by a number of factors, namely; land and pastures, the farmers' income, the milk market, inputs, climate, the type of cattle breed, veterinary care, methods of grazing, water availability and farm management practices. In contrast to earlier days when the government or farmers' cooperatives subsidised farm inputs, nowadays, farmers today have to purchase inputs from private supplies at commercial rates.

In some areas, however, farmers have formed new associations in response to changing state policies. In Bushenyi for example, farmers' co-operatives are being revived. Bushenyi Dairy Industries Company (BUDICO), a recently formed farmer's co-operative, is organising farmers and encouraging them to take a uniform position in bargaining for the price of milk with buyers. The move to reactivate co-operatives in Bushenyi is the result of the farmers' frustrations regarding their inability to determine milk prices. In areas where farmers have failed to organise, some of them have simply quit cattle farming altogether.

Although the production of raw milk at the farm level increased with the liberalisation of the economy, there was no corresponding expansion of the processing and marketing sub-sectors to absorb the massive upsurge in milk production. The consequent gap between supply and demand in Ankole was compounded by the closure of some of the factories. The increased operations milk hawkers coupled with the lack of a proper regulatory framework for the dairy sector which made it difficult for the processors to break even (see section 3.6.5). This created confusion in the supply chain due to poor governance. Eventually, many factories had to close. Meanwhile, milk production at the farm level continued to be plentiful, pushing prices downwards. This situation still prevails.

Currently, the low price of milk[21] vis-a-vis the high price of inputs increasingly makes it difficult for farmers to break even. As a result, farm management has suffered. Most farms visited during this study were in deplorable condition and in need of rehabilitation. The owners complained that due to low farm gate prices for raw milk it was too expensive to maintain their farms in good order.

Marketing outlets constitute another problem for farmers. Farmers in Ankole have no guaranteed markets for their surplus milk. Consumers and processors can pick and choose. It is a buyer's market. This leads to unpredictable price fluctuations[22]. In addition, the confusion and uncertainty in the milk market, especially in periods of excess supply, have depressed the farmers' incomes and diminished their capacity to modernise their farms. This volatile fluctuation in the price of milk has particularly affected farmers in areas such Nyabushozi, where a lot of milk is wasted especially during the rainy season when it is in great supply.

Several analysts, including Saamanya (2002) & Twinamasiko (2002), have noted that the cost of producing milk in Ankole is the lowest in Uganda and East Africa in general, mainly because the cattle are feed on natural pastures with limited farm inputs, including labour and maintenance costs. Farmers in Kenya, for instance, have to give supplements to their cattle and take additional care of their farm and animals, which makes the cost of producing a litre of milk much more expensive there than in Ankole. Ankole, therefore, has a comparative advantage and the potential to become a leading milk producing area in the East Africa region, if only all the production, processing and marketing challenges facing this sub-sector can be overcome. Milk marketing, in particular, remains a big challenge facing in Ankole, especially in this era of liberalisation.

Changes at the Farm Level

Changing Production Systems

There are three methods of cattle keeping in Ankole, namely; open-grazing, paddocking and zero-grazing. Open grazing has been Ankole's traditional practice especially in the extensive grasslands in the southern and eastern parts of the region. In this case, the farmland is often not paddocked, but the boundaries are fenced with a plant locally known as *oruyenje*. The daily routine of open grazing farmers is morning milking, grazing, watering evening milking and late evening grazing. Traditional husbandry activities still widely practiced in Nyabushozi including bonfire lighting for the cattle in the morning and in the evening to scare away flies (locally known as *"embu"*) and tsetse flies. Another activity is the provision of salt for cattle to lick.

Paddock grazing, on the other hand, is a common farming practice in areas where the land holdings are fairly small. This type of grazing requires land clearing and improved pasture. It is largely practiced by farmers of hybrid and cross-breed cattle and has expanded rapidly with the liberalisation of the economy which has resulted in the need to make farms economically viable. In order to increase production, some farmers, especially in Bushenyi, have planted legumes, elephant grass and alfalfa, for their cattle.

The zero-grazing refers to the confinement of a few animals in a small enclosure where feeds or fodder and water are brought to the animals. This practice has spread in Ankole with the liberalisation of the economy and the government distribution of free cattle, mainly to women groups and poor households under poverty eradication programmes. At least 20 per cent of the low-income households in Ankole have received a zero-grazing cow not only from government but also from such organisations as Send A Cow (UK) and the Heifer Project International[23]. The advantage of this grazing system is that people without much land for grazing are able to raise cattle to produce milk for home consumption and to earn an income. It also makes it easier for farmers to collect cow dung and urine for crop fertilization[24]. In Ankole, zero-grazing is mostly practiced in Igara, Sheema and Kashari counties.

Changes in Types of Cattle

Ankole is famous world wide for its long-horned cattle. Although no livestock census has been conducted recently to establish their actual numbers, it was clear from the research interviews that many farmers have increasingly taken up cross-breeds to boost milk production at the farm level. Out of the 105 farms visited during my field research, with a total of 9,423 heads of cattle, 41 per cent were Long-horned cattle, 38 per cent cross-breeds, while exotic and Boran breeds accounted for 19 per cent and 2 per cent, respectively (Table 3.2 & Figure 3.4).

Table 3.2: Number of Cows & Types for Selected Counties in Ankole

County	No. of farms visited	Total no. of Cows owned	Local	% Approx	Cross	% Approx	Exotic	% Approx	Boran	% Approx.
Nyabushozi	15	3,330	2,032	61	1,172	35	6	0	120	4
Kashari	15	1,840	155	8	824	45	791	43	70	4
Isingiro	15	1,262	633	50	629	50	-	-	-	-
Sheema	15	563	48	8	140	25	375	67	-	-
Igara	15	669	-	-	70	10	599	90	-	-
Rubaare	15	769	462	60	283	37	24	3	-	-
Ruhaama	15	990	532	54	428	43	30	3	-	-
Totals	105	9,423	3,862	41	3,546	38	1,825	19	190	2

Source: Authors' Fieldwork May 2003

In Nyabushozi county in Mbarara district, as in Ruhama and Rubaare counties in Ntungamo district, the long-horned Ankole cattle represented 61 per cent of the cattle owned by the respondents (Table 4.2). This is largely so because the Nyabushozi dry savanna grasslands has a lot of pests and diseases and is not yet conducive to cross or exotic breeds of cattle. The area is nonetheless favourable to the local long horned Ankole cattle, which are more resistant to pests and can survive longer without much water. The landholdings in Nyabushozi are considerably larger than those in other parts of Ankole. The land belonging to all the farmers interviewed in Nyabushozi was over 100 acres each.

Figure 3.4 Percentages of Cattle Breeds in Ankole

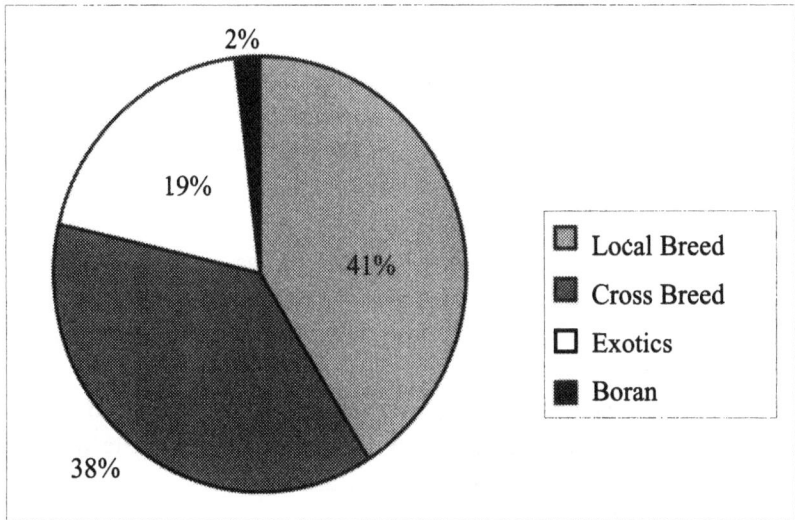

Source: Author's Fieldwork May 2003

In contrast, the average land holding for farmers interviewed in parts of Igara and Sheema was approximately 20 hectares. This explains why farmers in Bushenyi practice intensive farming with paddocking and the cultivation of fodder crops.

It should be mentioned, however, that in Nyabushozi, the local breed is gradually being transformed by cross-breeding to get more milk and earn more income. From the 15 farmers interviewed in Nyabushozi, only one was keeping pure local breeds exclusively. Apart from two families, new cross-breeds started being acquired beginning at the 1988[25] when the NRM government began to liberalise the economy, including the milk industry. The opening up of the economy therefore expanded demand for milk and this encouraged farmers to acquire cross or high-breed cattle to produce more milk. In addition, the gradual establishment of milk factories in Mbarara town took place around this time and this too stimulated the demand for cross and exotic cattle breeds[26].

However, local administrative officials interviewed in the area contended that a sizeable number of local farmers in Nyabushozi are still very conservative in that they prefer to keep the local long-horned cattle because they multiplied faster and that although they gave little milk, the milk was very nutritious. For them, the sale of milk is not a priority because they obtain their income from the sale of cattle. The fact that the local cattle are resistant to diseases like East Coast fever and inflamation of teats[27] also explains many Bahima prefer local breeds, which do not need as much farm inputs in form of drugs and accaricides as cross and exotic breeds. Also, for many Bahima the Ankole long-horned cattle are traditional symbols of social status.

The situation is different in Igara and Sheema in Bushenyi district, which were the first areas in Ankole to adopt hybrid cattle in the 1960s. The field study showed that in Isingiro the proportion of local breeds is equal to that of cross breeds (50 per cent each). It is worth noting that, exotic farmers in Rubare, Ruhaama, Isingiro and Nyabushozi lag behind their Igara and Sheema counterparts because the keeping of cross-breeds started in the 1960s (see Table 3.3).

Table 3.3: Period when Selected Farmers in Milk producing Areas of Ankole Started Keeping Cross & Hybrid Cattle

	1960s	1970s	1980s	Btn 1986-1993	After 1993
Nyabushozi	1	1	2	2	9
Kashari	6	2	3	1	3
Isingiro	-	1	5	6	5
Sheema	9	2	1	2	1
Igara	10	1	-	2	2
Rubaare	-	1	1	8	5
Ruhaama	1	1	2	7	4

Source: Author's Fieldwork May 2003

Changes in Milk Production Levels

Milk productivity levels have also been changing since liberalisation of the economy. For example, whereas milk from Ankole totalled approximately 150 million litres in 1992, it rose to approximately 350 million by 1999 and was estimated at approximately 350 million in 2001 (DDA Annual report 2001). This, as noted earlier, is largely due to the acquisition of cross and hybrid cattle by an increasing number of dairy farmers in Ankole. The establishment of milk processing plants in Ankole also gave many farmers the impetus to increase productivity initially but ultimately over the years, the closure of these factories and increasing marketing problems, has led to a glut of milk in Ankole. This explains why farm gate prices have continuously dropped and why milk marketing has become a serious problem in Uganda.

However, it was interesting to learn during my field research that, among the selected farmers visited, the number of milking cows on each farm is relatively small. Out of the 105 farms visited with 9,423 cows, only 2,107 cows (22 per cent) were being milked that is, lactating [See Table 3.4]. The farmers indicated that lactating cows need a lot more care and, as such, they can only manage to care for a few at a time. This indicates there is still potential for increased productivity.

Table 3.4: Lactating Cows in Selected Areas of Ankole

County	Total Farms visited	Total no. of cows owned	Lactating cows	Percentage (Approx.)
Nyabushozi	15	3,330	495	15
Kashari	15	1,840	525	29
Isingiro	15	1,262	280	23
Igara	15	669	267	40
Sheema	15	563	220	39
Ruhaama	15	990	197	20
Rubaare	15	769	123	16
Total	105	9,423	2,107	22

Source: Authors' Fieldwork May 2003

In order to maximise milk production, dairy farmers ideally ought to know the milking history of their cows. In practice, this has not been the case. In the 1960s, farmers used to acquire genuine breeds from government farms, but with the liberalisation of the economy, farmers have to buy cows on the open market without knowing their history. In some cases, farmers have been ripped off by unscrupulous businessmen who sell breeds that are not genuine milkers. Many farmers complained about this during the research.

Data collected during the field research shows that the mean literage among cross and exotic breeds in Ankole is 9.4 litres, ranging from the highest milker, which is 17.6 litres, to the lowest, which is 1.1 litres. For the local breeds, the mean literage is 0.95 litres, ranging from 1.8 litres to 0.1 litres (see Table 3.5).

Table 3.5: Milk Productivity Levels in Ankole

County	Total No. of farms vis- ited	Cross/exotic breeds			Local breeds			Milk production		
		Best milker (lts)	Low- est milker (lts)	Aver- age	Best milker (lts)	Low- est milker (lts)	Aver- age	Prod. per day (lts)	Sold Per day (lts)	Retai- ned at home (lts)
Nyabushozi	15	8.5	3	5.8	1.6	0.7	1.2	2,624	2,350	274
Kashari	15	10.3	4.1	7.2	1.3	0.3	0.8	2,892	2,199	683
Isingiro	15	4.5	1.5	3.0	1.8	0.3	1.1	759.5	501	258.5
Igara	15	17.6	9.6	13.6	-	-	-	2,490	2,155	312
Sheema	15	13.8	6.2	10.0	0.4	0.1	0.3	1,254	785	469
Rubaare	15	2.8	1.1	1.9	1.1	0.2	0.6	496	316	180
Ruhaama	15	3.5	1.2	2.4	1.1	0.2	0.6	612	470	142
Total	105	61	26.7	43.8	7.3	1.8	4.5	11,128	8,776	2,318.5
Average milker		8.7	3.8		1	0.3				

Source: Authors' Fieldwork May 2003

According to Mr Rugunda, one of the prominent farmers in Mbarara, when he imported exotic breeds from the Netherlands, the milk prices were high enough for him to maintain his farm well. On average each imported milking cow produced 30 litres. This again shows that, despite the increasing levels of milk production in Ankole, the yield per cow is still low.

By simple arithmetic, the number of cows in Nyabushozi generally outweighs the quantity of milk produced. The total number of cows owned by the 15 farmers interviewed was 3,330. Only 495 (15 per cent) were lactating, producing a total quantity of 2,624 litres per day. The situation is different in Bushenyi District. In Igara, for instance, out of a total of 669 cows, 267 (40 per cent), were lactating and producing 2,490 litres in all. These figures suggest that encouraging farmers to adopt cross-breeds in the whole of Ankole would increase milk production, provided a clear supply chain is to be established to ensure the milk is marked. In Kashari, too, the average milk yield amount per cow is increasing with the improvement of paddock grazing and farming practices.

Some indigenous cattle breed owners in Rubaare, Ruhaama and Nyabushozi, do not milk some of their cows at all on the grounds that they prefer to raising healthy offsprings for sale and breeding to selling small quantities of milk at give away prices. Farmers realise that well-fed calves grow quickly and hence fetch higher prices and consequently, better income in a shorter period of time.

Milk quality on the farm

The quality of milk is one of the critical elements in the flow of milk from the producer to the consumer. Unfortunately, the quality of milk from Ankole dairy farmers is generally poor due to hand milking, unhygienic handling and adulteration with water. The quality of milk appears to have deteriorated during liberalisation of the economy. With liberalisation, many actors have rushed into the commercial milk sub-sector without the requisite knowledge, technical expertise, professional competence and integrity to handle milk for human consumption.

On the farm, the quality of milk is affected by a number of factors, including the health of the cattle, the handling of the milk, the hygiene of the milker, the type of feeds, water sources[28] and transportation. The quality of milk is determined by the level of its microbial content. According to the District Veterinary Officer in Mbarara, if milk comes from a healthy animal and good hygiene has been practices, the microbial content should be very low. But if the milk is from an unhealthy animal or handled unhygienically, then its microbial content will be high.

In Ankole, most farmers are either ignorant of the need to ensure high milk quality right from the farm. For example, with the exception of Bushenyi, in most of the areas covered by this study, farmers indicated they do not wash the udders of cows before milking. They assume that allowing the calf to suckle before milking is sufficient to clean the teats. Bad milking practices were observed on some farms in Nyabushozi and Ntungamo where the milkers dipped his dirty fingers into the milk in order to lubricate the cows teats while milking.

Farmers also use dirty containers which contaminate the milk. The most common milking vessels used in Ankole are aluminium pails or plastic buckets, though the Bahima traditionally use wooden milking vessels known as *ebyanzi*. They smoke these vessels with a plant known as *olea africana* to give the milk a particular flavour and this tends to contaminate the milk[29]. Without thorough cleanliness of the milking cows, the milk man and the milk containers, it is difficult to ensure high quality milk from the dairy farms.

It was also observed on many farms visited that milk men do not wash their hands before milking. Sometimes the teats are smeared with cow dung after milking *okuhomera* as a means of preventing teat rush. This is a common practise particularly among farmers with indigenous breeds. On the next milking, the cow is given its calf for suckling and milking follows without cleaning the teats. The saliva from the calves' mouth and the unwashed teats contaminates the milk[30].

In addition, apart from Bushenyi where dairy farmers have constructed well-maintained milking shades or parlours the common practice in most parts of Ankole is to milk in open spaces with a bucket or other containers. This means that when a cow urinates or defecates in the course of milking some of the urine or dung particles may drop into the milk. Also, if milking takes place when it is raining, rain drops may fall into the milk and contaminate it. Moreover, dirty milking places tend to be infested with flies, some of which may fall into the milk causing contamination.

Figure 3.5: Hand Milking in an Enclosure in Isingiro

In the past, the government used to offer training to dairy farmers. Following liberalisation however, much of this training has been left to the NGOs which do not operate everywhere. Consequently, milk produced on the farm in Ankole is of very poor quality. The exception is only in Bushenyi district where NGO training efforts have been concentrated and where farmers have been more respective to the best practices for farm management.

Changing Institutional Frameworks

At the moment there is no clear code of conduct that farmers must follow to ensure the production of good quality milk on their farms. The changing institutional framework within which these farmers are now operating has also aggravated the problem of milk quality in Ankole.

a) The Fall and Rise of Co-operatives

The destruction of co-operatives has negatively affected the milk industry in Ankole. As noted earlier, successive governments since the 1960s partly saw the co-operative movement as an instrument of control and an informal mechanism through which rural surplus could be extracted for the benefit of the urban dwellers while at the same time, improving the incomes and quality of life of rural communities. However, the co-operative system was abused and co-operatives lost the purpose for which they were created. Cronyism became rampant and often the hard earned savings of society members were misappropriated. The co-operative movement in Ankole, as elsewhere in the country, became completely discredited in the eyes of the farmers. The Obote II government attempted to revive co-operatives and dairy farmers in Ankole for sometime began to reap some benefits. With the onset of liberalisation however, most of these quasi-government co-operatives were dismantled leaving many farmers in disarray, especially with regard to milk marketing[31] since a perishable commodities cannot be economically marketed on an individual basis and require co-operation between the farmers. Eventually, the NRM government in recognition of the importance of co-operatives revised co-operative societies statute in 2002.

In the milk industry, co-operatives are therefore being revived to enable farmers to negotiate better prices for their milk. Such co-operatives can among other things, negotiate fair benefit from bulk purchase discounts, prices and purchase farm inputs in bulk for farmers to arrange training for farmers. Co-operatives give farmers a collective voice. Dairy farmers nationwide have registered a new co-operative named Uganda National Farmers Union (UNFAU) whose primary objective is to buy DCL, which is currently being privatised.

Furthermore, in some areas like Bushenyi and Nyabushozi, efforts are underway to revive and strengthen co-operatives in marketing activities. BUDICO, for instance, an umbrella organisation for dairy farmers in Bushenyi, currently has 19 collecting centres with coolers and five collecting sub-centres without coolers[32]. One of its major objectives is to advocate fair milk prices for the farmers, improve the quality of animals and farms and to act as a collective voice for farmers. Ankole Dairy Products (ADAP), a farmer's co-operative in Rushere, is endeavouring to expand its membership in Nyabushozi and mobilise farmers to work together to ensure the efficient marketing of their milk. In Ntungamo too, farmers are mobilising themselves to engage more in marketing their milk. It is only in Kashari county that no well-established farmers organisation could be identified, but even then, some NGOs like Land O' Lakes are educating and encouraging farmers to form co-operatives.

In areas where co-operatives have been revived, farmers are beginning to reap profits in terms of more stable prices and regular payments. In my interview with Mr Makaru, the chairman of BUDICO, it was established that farmers in Bushenyi have negotiated a fixed price for their milk throughout the year and a guarantee to buy all the milk that is collected. This has made farmers' incomes more predictable than they used to be. BUDICO has also negotiated a contract arrangement with DCL to supply high quality milk.

b) Privatisation of Veterinary Services

In its Plan for Modernisation of Agriculture, the NRM has endorsed the privatisation of veterinary services but this, according to many veterinarians, may turn out to be very problematic and costly. The limited number of private veterinary doctors in the private sector often do not have adequate equipment and resources to render veterinary services effectively. The cost of offering proper veterinary services is very high. For example, veterinary private practitioners need laboratories to properly analyse livestock samples but the cost of installing and maintaining such laboratories is prohibitive for most individuals. Therefore, most of the cattle treatments especially in rural areas is based on local experience and guesswork. Laboratory findings and post mortems do not exist. Moreover, since most farmers cannot afford veterinary services, they resort to 'do it yourself' diagnoses, treatments and other remedies.

On the whole, veterinary services at the farm level have been very ineffective and all the farmers visited highlighted inefficiency as a major weakness on the part of government. Out of the 15 farms visited in Isingiro, 60 per cent had never seen an extension worker or veterinary officer (see Table 3.6). In contrast, on-farm visits were more frequent in Sheema, Igara and Kashari, which explains why farmers in Bushenyi have adopted better farm management practices than anywhere else in Ankole.

Before liberalisation, government provided veterinary services through the line ministry. Veterinary doctors were posted in each district with several veterinary assistants attached to the officer and these often conducted on-farm visits subsidised fees. With liberalisation, however, the government sought to privatise the veterinary services even though government-paid veterinary doctors were posted at counties to deal with non-clinical issues.

Table 3.6: Frequency of Farm Visits by an Extension Workers or Veterinary Doctors on Selected Farms in Ankole.

County	No. of respo-ndents	At least once a month	%ge	At least once in three months	%ge	At least once in six months	%ge	At least once a year	%ge	Never at all	%ge
Nyabushozi	15	1	7	2	13	3	20	2	13	7	47
Kashaari	15	1	7	3	20	5	33	4	27	2	13
Isingiro	15	0	-	2	13	1	7	3	20	9	60
Igara	15	1	7	3	20	5	33	2	13	4	27
Sheema	15	1	7	4	27	3	20	5	33	2	13
Rubaare	15	0	-	1	7	2	13	5	33	7	47
Ruhaama	15	0	-	2	13	1	7	4	27	8	53
Totals	105	4	4	17	16	20	19	25	24	39	37

Source: Authors' Fieldwork May 2003

Unfortunately, in Ankole as in many other cattle keeping areas of Uganda, access to proper veterinary services is a serious problem. Farmers at times are not aware that a cow is ill. This ignorance, coupled with the lack of proper veterinary assistance, means that many cows go for long periods without being treated and this has an impact on the quality of their milk [33].

Last but not least, with the liberalisation of the economy, drugs are now available everywhere downside, however, is that "do it yourself" farmers tend to administer drugs without any professional guidance. They also do not observe the withdrawal periods[34] and continue to milk a cow that is undergoing treatment. This also impacts negatively on the milk quality and could be a health hazard to the consumer.

c) The Phasing out of Government training Institutes

Lack of awareness on the part of the farmers is a cause for concern with regard to maintaining milk quality on farms. Farming is an art, but most farmers in Ankole lack know-how. This has resulted in poor farm management and ultimately poor milk quality. Treatments for cattle are not well administered and this has a negative impact on the health of the cow and subsequently the milk. The high price of drugs further worsens the situation as farmers are inclined to under-dose their animals to minimise the quantities of the drugs they use without regard of the long-term consequences for animal health and disease control.

Bushenyi District has the highest level of farmers who have received training by either government or NGOs in the last five years. Of the farmers visited in Igara county, 47 per cent had received some training in the last five years, while in Sheema it was 53 per cent. This may also explain why the quality of milk from Bushenyi is better than that of other parts of Ankole. In Nyabushozi, Rubare and Ruhaama, the majority of the farmers (53 per cent, 60 per cent and 60 per cent, respectively) indicated that they had never received any formal training in animal husbandry or farm management.

In general terms, a high percentage of farmers in Ankole (51 per cent) have neither the formal training nor the skills necessary for operating commercial farms or keeping cattle. Only 30 per cent have had some training in the last five years, while only 19 per cent had been trained more than 5 years ago (Figure 3.5).

Figure 3.5: Farmers who have attained training in Ankole

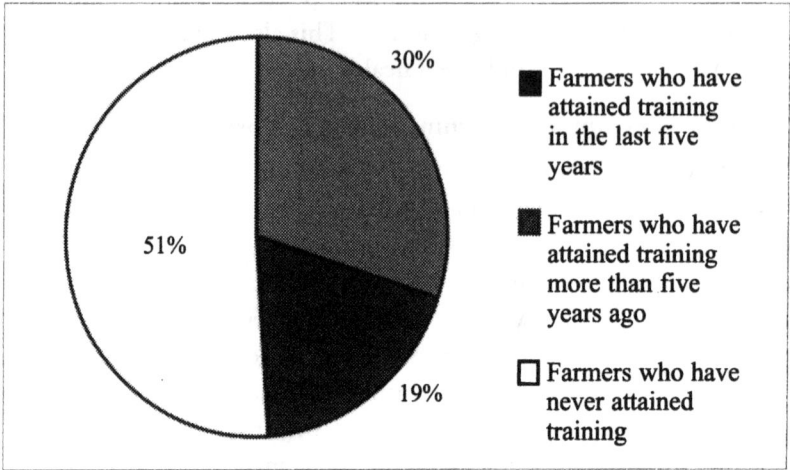

Women and Dairying in Ankole

Traditionally, cattle keeping in Ankole has been the role of men. Occasionally, young girls would assist in taking cattle for grazing, but this practice is limited to the Bahima. The role of women in dairy production in Ankole has changed significantly since the early 1990s when Heifer Project International (HPI), an international NGO introduced a zero-grazing project in Ankole to be operated by women. The aim was to help women provide milk for the families and earn an income through the sale of milk. This project was first implemented in Bushenyi District on a pilot basis before extending to small women groups in Mbarara and Ntungamo districts. Under this project, more than 100 woman in Bushenyi, mostly widows and the under-privileged, have benefited[35]. Other organisations like Send-A Cow (UK) and the various churches have since launched similar activities.

These projects have involved women in the dairy industry. Under these projects, women are trained in livestock management to enable them manage their animals and contribute to the general welfare of their families and communities. To sustain and spread the projects, each beneficiary is required to pass on a female offspring of her cow to another woman farmer. In areas like Bwongera and Kyangyenyi villages in Bushenyi that have benefited from these initiatives, women have proved to better accountability than men and spread the benefits to their families better than their male counterparts.

However, there are several other areas where men have supported women. In Ankole, as in most parts of Uganda, married women do not own land. Normally, the land is under the control of the husband and this practice has inhibited many women from taking part in these projects. One such woman, Mrs Kentengye, from Kyangyengi Women's Group in Bushenyi who was interviewed during my research study, received a heifer in 1993 from HPI. She had to get her husband's permission to get involved in the project and then had to turn to him for financial support to sustain the cow, as she had no initial capital of her own.

Following these initiatives, some women groups in Ankole have established their own well managed zero grazing schemes by pooling resources together successfully and offering their families improved incomes and better nutrition.

In conclusion to this section, it is quite evident that liberalisation has brought about a number of changes in the milk industry, at the farm level and beyond. A lot of farm management practices and dynamics are changing. The revival of co-operatives, for instance, is seen as a worthwhile undertaking that promises to enable farmers to address their milk marketing problems. More areas in Ankole need to respond likewise. Farmers in Ankole have increasingly adopted hybrid cattle and this has among other things, substantially increased farm management and input costs, making it more expensive for dairy farmers in Ankole to maintain economically viable farms.

Although farmers indicated that there was a marked improvement immediately after the liberalisation process began and in particular when private milk dairies sprung up in Mbarara, the entry of more farmers in the business coupled with marketing problems led to an over-supply of raw milk. The closure of most of the factories and the resultant fall in prices has disillusioned farmers in Ankole who originally saw dairy farming as a profitable and sustainable economic activity. Farmers face with numerous challenges, which affect the quality of their milk. These challenges had a negative impact on the movement of milk from the production to marketing. This will be discussed further in detail in the next section.

Milk Marketing and Processing Dynamics and Changes

Milk marketing in Ankole has undergone tremendous changes with the onset of liberalisation and various actors are now involved in milk processing and marketing. This section presents an assessment of the supply chains around milk processing and marketing by highlighting the changing governance structures and institutional frameworks and their effects on the performance of the milk industry in the era of liberalisation. It also highlights the challenges arising from hawkers.

Milk Sale in Ankole

In Ankole, there are three categories of milk buyers and vendors. The first category are the bicycle vendors who buy milk from the farmers and sell it from house to house. Secondly, there are the licensed traders who own coolers and sell milk on wholesale or retail basis. Then there are the established and licensed processors who process, pack and sell milk to consumers in Masaka or Kampala where the demand for milk is high. It should be mentioned here that many farmers in Ankole still sell their milk directly to consumers. Private marketing agents and processors handle only approximately 40 per cent of this produce[36].

The milk traders can be sub-divided into two categories, namely licensed traders who often transport milk to major urban centres and unlicensed milk vendors who sell fresh milk door to door. Together, these two types of traders command the largest share of the milk market in Ankole (over 80 per cent).

The milk marketing chains in Ankole, therefore, are twofold: that is, the processed milk chain and the unprocessed milk chain. The characteristics of both processed and unprocessed[37] milk chains are summarised in Table 5.1. The boundaries between the two chains are at times porous and are continuously shifting[38]. The processed milk chain is more efficient than the unprocessed milk one.

Table 5.1: Key Characteristics of the Milk Chains in Ankole

Processed Milk Chain	Unprocessed Milk Chain
• Test the raw milk at the farm level to ensure quality	• Do not usually test the milk and quality not an issue
• Largely use modern methods to preserve the milk and quality is an important issue	• Uses traditional methods like boiling to preserve milk
• Obtain fresh milk from key established suppliers	• Obtain milk from any source
• Maintain contact and collaborate with suppliers	• Often have no attachment to supplier
• Deal in processed milk with a longer shelf life	• Deal in raw milk with a very short shelf life

Since the vendors and some licensed traders have no regular suppliers, they receive milk of variable quality. However, the informal/ unprocessed milk chain is flexible enough to undercut the prices offered by the processors more regular and upfront through payments. In addition, given their lower overhead costs, vendors and licensed traders have managed to outcompete the formal/processed milk chain and this has constrained the growth of the milk industry.

My field research with the smaller farmers showed that they usually opt to supply the vendors who pay cash on delivery. These vendors have in some instances provided such inducements as cheaper milk cans to farmers to ensure regular supplies and maintain the farmers' loyalty. The major complaint of farmers against the vendors was about the frequent fluctuation in price of the raw milk. In Ntungamo and Mbarara districts, for instance, the daily prices offered by vendors and milk traders varied and changed more than six times during the period of three months research (July to September 2002), ranging from Ug Sh 100/= to Ug Sh 280/= per litre. To many farmers, these fluctuations were very frustrating because without predictable incomes farmers could not plan for acquisition of farm inputs and other improvements.

The processors, on the other hand, have found it necessary to identify and sign contracts in order to ensure particular farmers supply good quality raw milk. DCL, for instance, has contracted BUDICO to collect 15,000 litres of milk per day and deliver it to its processing plant in Kampala. All processors are particular about the quality of milk obtained from the farm level and undertake several tests before they accept it from the farmers. Because of the perishable nature of milk, there is need for strict quality control right from the farm level through collecting and on to processing – a very delicate part of the formal supply chain. There are only two major processors currently operating in Mbarara with DCL only buying milk from Ankole.

DCL, still controls the bulk of the milk collection in Ankole and its supply chain is fairly systematic. It has a better network of collecting centres with coolers and has recently improved its payment methods to farmers. Although the government is now in the process of divesting it, DCL still operates as a parastatal. It has several milk collecting centres in most of the major trading centres in the largest milk producing counties in Ankole, which are manned by farmers' co-operatives. Members of these cooperatives deliver the milk to the collection centres. DCL then uses its refrigerated vehicles to collect and deliver it to its major milk depot in Mbarara, where it is chilled. From here, larger refrigerated vehicles transport the milk to Kampala for processing into a variety of milk products, including UHT milk, cheese, yoghurt and ice-cream.

Milk processors in Ankole operate much in the same way as DCL. They identify their own suppliers and agree to pay them a premium price, which is usually a bit higher than DCL's and more stable than the vendors' prices[39]. Farmers who supply processors agree on the minimum number of litres to be supplied per day at an agreed constant price (irrespective of the fluctuations elsewhere) for a specific period of time. Payments are often made at the end of the month. In most cases, however, the processor collects the milk from the farmer. Such formal, established arrangements were common amongst the larger farmers in Ankole with the better-established farms usually producing over 200 litres of milk per day. Most of these farms are located in Bushenyi district, though quite a number of such farms exist in Mbarara district as well.

Generally, milk marketing depends on a number of factors namely; infrastructure, laws and regulations, prices, taxation, information, quality control, credit/loan availability, co-operatives, research, extension services and culture. The next section analyses some of these factors in the context of the milk industry in Ankole.

Milk Sales by Co-operatives

Milk marketing has always been one of the most daunting problems of milk producers in Ankole and has become even more problematic since liberalisation. From the field research conducted in various parts of Ankole, it was observed that a sizeable number of the farmers sell their milk through farmers' co-operatives or associations (31 per cent), while others sell it individually [see Figure 5.1].

Figure 5.1:   Milk Delivery / Supply by Farmers

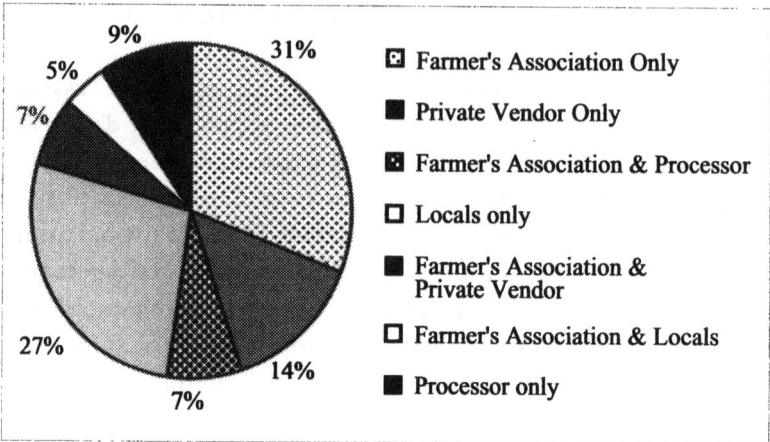

Legend:
- Farmer's Association Only — 31%
- Private Vendor Only
- Farmer's Association & Processor
- Locals only
- Farmer's Association & Private Vendor
- Farmer's Association & Locals
- Processor only

(Values shown on chart: 31%, 14%, 7%, 27%, 7%, 5%, 9%)

Source: Author's Fieldwork, March 2003.

Milk Sales by Individual Farmers

The milk that individual farmers sell at the farm level is influenced by price, quality and availability of buyers or collecting centres. In areas like Kashari and Isingiro, that lack co-operatives, milk marketing is a very serious problem. Farmers market their milk from the farm in three different ways. Farmers within vicinity of a collecting centre with a cooler often hire porters on a monthly basis to deliver the milk. Those located far from collecting centres, sell their milk to vendors or traders who in turn sell it to consumers. The third marketing procedure involves the milk processors who directly collect the milk from large-scale farms, producing substantial quantities of milk everyday.

A prominent large-scale farmer in Mutonto, Kashari, indicated that he was contracted by a private processor (GBK) to supply 300 litres of milk daily, on the understanding that the processor collects the milk from the farm. He also indicated that he had received some limited assistance in the form of milk cans and subsidised drugs, as well as on-farm training, from GBK. As noted earlier, some processors have devised innovative strategies to support their key suppliers and ensure that the latter remain loyal. Such an arrangement is very necessary in today's highly competitive market. In the era of liberalisation, therefore, private processors have stepped forward to provide farmers with some of the services previously offered by the state, but this assistance is only possible for those farmers that clearly comply with set standards of supplying good high quality milk. This is a clear change in the governance structure of the milk supply chain in Ankole.

In Nyabushozi, Isingiro and Ruhaama, however, there was another distinct form of arrangement or supply chain whereby milk buyers chose an agent from the farmers, paid him a commission and requested him to collect milk on their behalf. The agent is often given a commission of Ug Sh. 500 per 20 litres of milk. In order to collect as much milk as possible milk hawkers tended to attach more importance to quantity than quality. According to the production manager of GBK Dairies, these areas did not produce good quality milk and because most farmers are not organised in co-operatives (unlike Bushenyi), the price for milk here is dictated by the agents. Most of the farmers interviewed in these areas felt powerless and wished the government could intervene. The price of milk there fluctuates often and farmers have no guarantee that their milk will be bought daily since the agents collect milk on a first-come first-served basis and pay cash on delivery. According to some farmers interviewed in these areas, the hawkers not only agree on the milk price but they allocate themselves collection areas. Once an agent buys milk in a certain area, the others do not go there. Through this arrangement buyers enjoy a monopoly position and dictate prices to farmers desperate to sell their perishable milk.

In some parts of Ankole, particularly in Kashari, farmers indicated that they supplied different buyers at different times. In Mbarara district as a whole, 75 per cent of the farmers indicated that they supply milk to DCL in the mornings and to private vendors or hawkers in the evenings. In other words, they do not want to "put all their eggs in one basket." Many farmers in Mbarara have also been disillusioned following the closure of some milk processing factories. As one farmer put it, "you tap here and tap there hoping that if one trader or processor runs bankrupt and withdraws, then you have another to fall back"[40].

From the perspective of the farmer, milk marketing is clearly very problematic. Except in areas where co-operatives have been revived the flow of milk from the farm to the consumer is not smooth. While the price of milk has remained low, the costs of production risen. Several reasons have been given to explain the kinds of bottlenecks that exist along the milk chain (see section 5).

Price Fluctuations

Following the liberalisation of the economy, farm gate prices for milk have fluctuated in Ankole (and elsewhere in the country), particularly in areas with no co-operatives. The unit price of milk is also very low. In all my interviews, the respondents repeatedly complained about low prices. Mr Mugisha of Ruhaama, Ntungamo District, for instance, said he feels cheated when a litre of milk is sold for a maximum of Ug sh 300 compared to Ug sh 500 for a 250mls bottle (quarter a litre) of mineral water. He wondered why government can not educate the population about the importance of drinking more milk. On his part, Bishop Bamunoba of Kashari, Mbarara district, now an avid milk producer, wondered why people are willing to pay Ug sh 500 for a bottle of 200 mls of Coca-Cola which is less nutritional than an equal quantity of milk. Yet a litre of milk costs much less. He was disappointed by the government's failure to educate the population about the need to drink milk instead of fizzy drinks. The farmers' concerns point to the fact that the government needs to intervene in stabilising milk prices in order to sustain milk production.

In all areas of Ankole visited during this study, the prices offered for milk fluctuate from season to season. During the rainy season when there is plenty of water and pasture, the cost of milk is low and declines to about Ug sh 100 per litre or less, but in the dry season it rises to Ug sh 300/=, due to short falls in milk production resulting from the scarcity of water and pasture for cattle (see Table 5.1). Except for BUDICO farmers in Bushenyi and for the recently formed Ankole Dairy Products (ADAP) farmers' co-operative in Rushere, there is no fixed minimum price of milk in most parts of Ankole which means that farmers cannot predict their incomes and plan accordingly.

Another related issue, which contributes to the irregular prices of milk at the farm level, is that of the "manipulative" buyer. According to some respondents, during the rainy season, when milk is plentiful, milk hawkers often reject the farmers' milk on the ground that it is contaminated. Since these hawkers' do not complain about contamination during the dry season, it is reasonable to suppose that the real reason is over-supply which makes it possible for buyers to pick and choose and to push down prices. Farmers claimed that some buyers deliberately contaminate the milk through the use of unhygienic measuring instruments. Also buyers preferred to reject milk on grounds of quality (low fat content) rather than over-supply[41]. Some wise farmers, however, have foiled this trick.

Lack of clear governance structures to regulate the sale of milk in most parts of Ankole has created a lot of disorganisation in the marketing of milk right from the farm level. Individual farmers are being exploited because they produce a perishable commodity. Buyers have taken advantage of this situation to buy milk cheaply and consequently to depress farmers' incomes.

Unprocessed Milk Traders and Vendors in Ankole

Under liberalisation, traders and vendors of unprocessed milk have become a force to reckon within the milk industry in Ankole[42]. Their number has increased rapidly and they now control about 80% of the milk trade in Ankole, as indeed elsewhere in the country. Milk vendors and licensed milk traders transport the raw milk in low cost containers; mainly in plastic jerry cans (See Figure 5.4). Vendors mostly use bicycles for transport while traders use pick-ups or small trucks.

Figure 5.4: Transportation of Milk in Jerrycans by a Milk Trader in Ankole

Source: Author's Fieldwork 2003

As noted above, both these milk hawkers get the milk directly from the farmers and sell it to consumers either door to door (for the vendors), or in the major towns and urban centres (particularly Kampala), for licensed milk traders. The latter usually employ agents at certain key points along the main roads connecting various trading centres in the milk rich regions, to collect the milk from farmers and pay for it in cash. The milk is then transported in open pick-up trucks to either Mbarara or straight to Kampala. Most of the traders prefer to ferry the raw milk to Kampala but they also sell some of it in urban centres like Masaka, along the Mbarara-Kampala highway. Vendors, on the other hand, are found in every part of the region. They usually buy the milk from the farmers directly or from milk traders and then sell or distribute it to their customers on bicycles or motorcycles. The main challenge facing the traders of raw milk is to transport it to the major urban areas as quickly as possible and resell it before it goes bad. Since approximately 80 per cent of the milk sold on the domestic market goes through such "informal" channels, the formal market will remain small because of poor transportation conditions, the lack of refrigerated trucks and proper storage facilities to ensure that milk remains fresh and maintains its quality.

Impact of Milk Hawkers on the Milk Industry

Traditionally, pastoralists and other cattle keepers in Ankole used to exchange milk for food or cash in neighbouring villages. This practice spread to the urban areas in the late 1970s, when the lone dairy processing plant began to experience financial difficulties. Since then, there has been a proliferation of milk hawking activities in urban centres, particularly in Mbarara, Bushenyi and Ntungamo towns. This is mainly due to the weak dairy processing sector/infrastructure, the premature liberalisation of the dairy sector and an unregulated dairy market

As noted earlier, with the coming to power of the NRM government, some measures were taken to revitalise the milk industry. In 1993 the Dairy Master Plan Study funded by DANIDA recommended 3 major reforms in the dairy sector, namely: the liberalisation of the dairy industry the creation of a regulatory-body/dairy-board and commercialisation and divestiture of Dairy Corporation.

The proposed reforms, however, were not implemented in their order of importance although the sequence was unhelpful to human development. First, the government opted to liberalise the dairy industry. However, the Dairy Board, which was to oversee development and regulation of the industry, was not put in place until 8 years later. In the meantime, milk traders took advantage of liberalisation to expand their trade in raw milk, ferrying it in plastic jerrycans over long distances to the urban centres. There was a rapid proliferation of milk boiling centres in the major towns, especially Kampala and the sale of loose milk dominated the market.

Furthermore, following the liberalisation of the dairy industry, many entrepreneurs became involved in the milk trade. Between 1994 and 2001, private investors set up over 10 new dairy processing plants countrywide, while in Ankole more than six plants were established by 1998. Many dealers joined the informal milk channel, setting up over 30 coolers in Mbarara, while in Kampala alone there were 235 coolers as of December 2001 (DDA Annual Report, 2002).

While processors pay farmers periodically, and more or less regularly, hawkers (i.e vendors and traders) pay cash on delivery. Besides, hawkers sometimes pay higher prices if and when necessary, thus they have steadily secured control over the milk supply chain in Ankole. Hawkers can afford to pay higher prices for raw milk at times because they do not incur any processing and packaging costs.

In addition, the largely poor urban population prefer cheap, albeit poor quality milk from hawkers, who conveniently deliver the milk at the consumers doorsteps. Urban demand has enabled hawkers to capture more than 80 per cent of the market for milk countrywide. The weak purchasing power of most urban dwellers means that they choose the product on the basis of price rather than its quality. In addition, some consumers lack the information to distinguish between good and bad quality milk. Milk hawkers revisit milk quality improvement measures for fear of losing market share and reducing profit margins.

Since most hawkers purchase raw milk directly from farmers on a cash-on-delivery (COD) basis, they are always assured of a steady supply. Product quality is not an issue to them and as such they do not invest in facilities for proper transportation and handling. They do not incur processing and packaging costs. They have a fairly efficient product distribution system of selling from door-to-door and even on credit to their urban customers. Several customers find it more convenient to receive milk at their homes, than to go looking for it at the processors' retail outlets, even if at times they know the vendors have adulterated it.

These hawkers have impacted negatively on the milk industry in Ankole and elsewhere in the country. All the processors interviewed and officials in the dairy industry concurred that hawkers represent the most difficult challenge facing the dairy industry in Ankole and Uganda today. They lack facilities for pasteurisation and hygienic milk handling and end up adulterating the milk with water and chemicals. This means that a larger section of the Ugandan population is in fact drinking very unhygienic and contaminated milk, prone to causing health hazards. Hawkers also transport milk in poor quality vessels like plastic jerrycans and boil this milk under very unhygienic conditions before they sell it to customers.

In response to the criticisms of processors and government agents, the hawkers interviewed for this study lamented that the government is against them and in favour of their rivals. They complained that they are always dismissed as villains yet they are also trying to make a livelihood. They noted that processors are only crying foul because they have failed to cope with the rigours of competition. They further complained that the government has not offered any assistance to the hawkers to improve their businesses but instead see them as a threat to the industry. They indicated that the government is blind to the fact that hawkers provide affordable milk to many customers nationwide. They appealed to government to be fair and support hawkers improve their businesses[43].

Given their informal role, hawkers cannot attract development credit to improve their businesses and milk supply chain, unless they become organised in working groups/associations. They are currently very difficult to supervise and quality standards monitoring is impossible, because they are neither registered nor operate in clearly designated premises/sites. Many hawkers have also defied the ban on the transportation of milk in jerrycans.

Furthermore, these hawkers cannot support an organised and elaborate nation-wide milk collection system because they are reluctant to invest in milk collection infrastructure. They collect just enough milk from Ankole and only buy what they can sell in a day because they do not have the capacity to preserve fresh milk for much longer.

For these milk traders transporting raw milk from the remotest parts of Ankole to Kampala (a distance of more than 400 km) in dirty plastic jerrycans, on open pick-up trucks and at temperatures ranging between 26^0 - 28^0 C for 4 to 6 hours, is a risky business. On arrival in Kampala, most of the milk is generally spoilt. To prevent further deterioration, the hawkers boil it as soon as it reaches Kampala. Boiling is done in big cooking pans, which can take up to 60 litres. Sodium bicarbonate is usually added to the milk before boiling to reverse acidity and prevent clotting, even when the milk is already bad.

The addition of large quantities of sodium bicarbonate before boiling milk goes beyond the limits acceptable for human consumption. Samples analysed by DDA have shown that sodium bicarbonate was added to the tune of 500 times the minimum allowed amount in foods fit for human consumption[44]. Sodium bicarbonate toxicity has been associated with a number of complications, including kidney damage in infants, stomach upsets and tooth decay.

Furthermore, the prolonged heating of milk leads to the denaturing of proteins and the loss of calcium. Hawkers boil the milk at temperatures close to 100^0C for more than 30 minutes. This results in the loss of up to 50 per cent of the proteins in the milk. In addition, although milk is one of the best sources for calcium, when milk is heated for long, the calcium in the milk forms a complex that sticks on to the surface of the cooking pans. Samples analysed by DDA also showed calcium reduction of up to 50 per cent[45].

Milk boiling centres are located in very unhygienic slums. The people that boil the milk do not wear clean, protective clothing. Boiling centres normally lack clean water and sanitary facilities. Because hygiene is generally very poor, the risks of recontamination of milk after boiling is very high.

Milk hawkers are evidently the product of an unregulated milk industry. Although regulatory bodies are now in place, the implementation of relevant regulations and reforms still need to be done in order to address an issues that are central to the thriving of the milk industry in Ankole and, indeed, nationwide, especially in this era of liberalisation.

Milk Processors in Ankole

Milk processors in Ankole can be categorised into two groups. On the one hand there are the large processors who use advanced technology in the production of milk and own big establishments using large volumes of milk, with organised systems for milk collection. On the other hand, there are the small processors or those producing under some form of cottage industry exclusively for the local market in Ankole, using relatively basic technology. It should be noted, however, that only two big private processors are currently operating in Mbarara. Although the government-owned DCL[46] is a major player in the milk industry in Ankole, with its largest raw milk-collecting depot in Mbarara, its processing plant is located in Kampala.

It is the big processors in Ankole who operate an organised system of milk handling, with milk collection centres in the countryside, mostly using milk trucks to transport the milk and processing and packaging it before marketing it. Yet, many have failed in this industry due to the lack of regulation, poor marketing strategies, competition from imported milk brands and the high costs of inputs, to mention but a few.

Following the liberalisation of the economy in 1992, six milk processing plants namely Ra-Milk, Country Taste Dairies, Everfresh Dairies, Paramount Dairies, GBK Dairies and DCL were operational in Ankole. However, with exception of GBK Dairies, located about 2 kms from Mbarara town and Alpha Dairies, which is located about 4 kms from the city centre, on the Mbarara – Kabale Road, the rest have recently closed down. Even these two serving large-scale processing plants are constrained by high production costs, small markets and stiff competition from the informal milk sector (See Figures 5.5 & 5.6).

There are also numerous small-scale processors who produce a variety of milk products. Most of the processors interviewed for this study indicated that they chose to locate their businesses in Mbarara due to the easy availability of raw, fresh milk and the ready market in town.

Figure 5.5 GBK Dairy Factory in Mbarara

Source: Author's Fieldwork 2003

Processors add value to milk and incur operating costs thus the milk retail prices are higher than the vendors' unprocessed milk prices. Until recently, the only vendors' inputs in the milk supply chain were transport and jerrycans[47]. Most of the milk processors collect the milk themselves directly from the farm, especially from the larger farmers who have some contract arrangement with the big processors to consistently supply at least 200 litres of high quality milk per day. Most of the larger milk suppliers interviewed in the region said they were dissatisfied with the prices they received from the processors. However, they preferred contract arrangements which undertook to buy all the milk produced on their farms at stable prices.

Figure 5.6 Alpha Dairy Factory in Mbarara

Source: Author's Fieldwork 2003

This is a new development in milk marketing in Ankole, which has come about with liberalisation of the milk industry. As noted before, farmers used to deliver their milk to UDC's collecting centres but, nowadays, processors have had to enter into contract arrangements especially with the larger milk producers, in order to buy high quality milk in order to sustain to their levels of operation.

Stiff competition from milk traders and vendors has forced milk processors especially the larger ones to reduce production, resulting in under-utilisation of their installed capacities and high operating overheads. In order to cover their costs, milk processors have increased the prices of their milk products which has depressed the demand for those products and created a glut of their products in the market.

In addition, the liberalisation of the economy has opened the local market to cheaper imported, fresh milk substitutes and transformed consumption habits[48]. The decline or stagnation of milk consumption in well-to-do households has negatively impacted on the growth of the milk industry in Ankole and Uganda in general.

In general terms, the supply chain in Ankole's dairy processing industry is shown in Figure 5.8. Milk is collected from contract farmers, like Mr Rugunda of Kashari and transported to the factory premises. Ordinarily, GBK has 24 collecting centres all over Ankole which increase to about 30 during the peak seasons. According to the production manager at GBK, there are five centres each, along the Kyenshama route and Kyabugimbi & Kashaka route; three centres long the Bwizibweera route; two centres along the Kibega route and nine centres in Ntungamo. Alpha dairies has fifteen collecting centres all over Ankole, which increase to twenty during peak season. The marketing manager Alpha Dairies indicated that they have two centres in Rushere, Bishese, Biharwe and Kitura in Mbarara district; Nyamisindo and Kyafora in Ntungamo district and Bushenyi town and Kabwohe in Bushenyi District. In remote areas milk is first collected at centres[49] from where it is ferried in bulk to the factory premises.

Figure 5.8: A Supply Chain for Milk Processing in Ankole

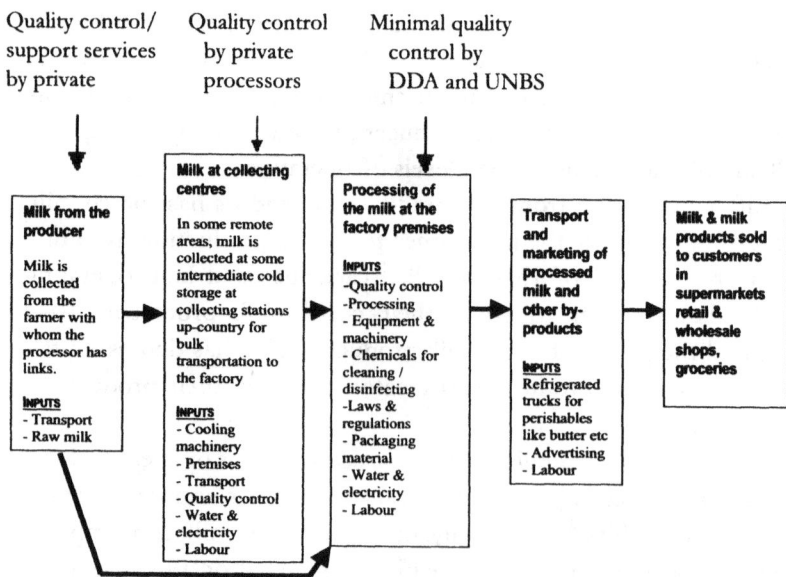

Quality control/ support services by private	Quality control by private processors	Minimal quality control by DDA and UNBS		
Milk from the producer	**Milk at collecting centres**	**Processing of the milk at the factory premises**	**Transport and marketing of processed milk and other by-products**	**Milk & milk products sold to customers in supermarkets retail & wholesale shops, groceries**
Milk is collected from the farmer with whom the processor has links.	In some remote areas, milk is collected at some intermediate cold storage at collecting stations up-country for bulk transportation to the factory			
INPUTS - Transport - Raw milk	**INPUTS** - Cooling machinery - Premises - Transport - Quality control - Water & electricity - Labour	**INPUTS** -Quality control -Processing - Equipment & machinery - Chemicals for cleaning / disinfecting -Laws & regulations - Packaging material - Water & electricity - Labour	**INPUTS** Refrigerated trucks for perishables like butter etc - Advertising - Labour	

Quality issues along the Milk Supply Chain for Milk Processors in Ankole

Quality problems run from the farmer to the consumer. Milk should have a sustained temperature of below 10^0c before being processed[50], but this is hardly adhered to in Ankole. As noted earlier, some milk is transported in unhygienic containers like plastic jerrycans. Although milk is usually tested for its fat content and possible adulteration, none of the milk factories in Mbarara has adopted a systematic and well-managed supply chain to ensure that good quality milk is produced at the farm level, collected in a hygienic manner, processed and packed in clean environment.

Figure 5.10 shows that farmers, largely because of lack of know-how, supply poor quality milk to the collecting centres the formal milk chain but here too, the persons supposed to test milk quality often lack the skills and the processors themselves do not handle milk in hygienic surroundings.

Figure 5.10: A Summarised version of the Flow of Quality Problems from the Farmer to the Consumer along the Formal milk Chain

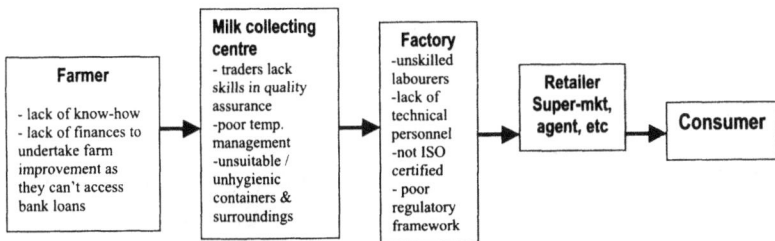

Farmer	Milk collecting centre	Factory	Retailer Super-mkt, agent, etc	Consumer
- lack of know-how - lack of finances to undertake farm improvement as they can't access bank loans	- traders lack skills in quality assurance -poor temp. management -unsuitable / unhygienic containers & surroundings	-unskilled labourers -lack of technical personnel -not ISO certified - poor regulatory framework		

Changing Policy and Institutional Framework for Milk Processing and Marketing

The official regulations for the dairy industry in Uganda are contained in the Dairy Industry Act of 1997, which gives powers to the DDA to regulate the industry. However, largely due to the lack of sufficient funds, DDA has not been able to perform its roles, including, the promotion of market research in dairy produce and the improvement in quality and promotion of private enterprise in production among the others. Milk processors in Mbarara indicated that DDA has been of no help to them other than its concentration on the policing role of quality inspections.

Generally, then, the institutional constraints affecting the dairy industry in Ankole and nationwide relate mainly to inadequate policies, out-dated laws and poor regulatory mechanisms. Arguably, the legal framework lagged behind the market liberalisation policy changes of the 1990s and this is what has destroyed the milk processing industry in Ankole[51]. For instance, although DDA now issues licenses to traders of raw milk, the regulations that were there before liberalisation (like disallowing trading in non-processed milk) are still in place.

The privatisation of extension and veterinary services under the Policy on Delivery of Veterinary Services (2001) has also had a negative impact on the quality of milk from the farm level to the processors. As already noted, there is now a low ratio of extension staff to farmers in all areas of Ankole with many farmers indicating they had not received any visits for the last year or so (see section 3.4.6). This has no doubt impacted negatively on the way in which farmers manage their farms. This explains why issues of low quality milk are pronounced in many areas of Ankole.

Another factor mentioned before but worth emphasising here is the poor transport network and impassable roads. Good logistics require good infrastructure. In most milk producing areas of Ankole, however, the road networks are only seasonally passable and rarely maintained, especially in Nyabushozi and Ruhaama. Instances of milk wastage especially during wet season are common in Ankole and as noted earlier, an estimated 30 per cent of milk production from these areas is lost annually due to the poor state of roads. This disrupts continuity in the milk supply chain in Ankole.

The lack of good and effective linkages to improve the livestock industry generally and the dairy industry in particular, as well as the sharing of information for dairy development, especially among national institutions, is another problem. Governance within the dairy industry is, in effect, deficient. Co-ordination between ministries and regulatory bodies and all other key actors in the milk industry is limited and in some cases, non-existent. During my field research, it was established that some of the NGO activities which assist farmers, for instance, are not known to the Ministry of Agriculture, Animal Industry and Fisheries because there is no coordination between the ministry and various NGOs. This has at times led to conflicts and duplication of tasks. There is need to foster and strengthen linkages with all the stakeholders to enhance sector governance, if the dairy industry is to be developed.

Taxation policy has also not been conducive to the development of the milk industry. Processors interviewed in Mbarara complained that taxes have been increasing since commencement of their business, eating into their profits and making it difficult to break even. High taxes make the import of spare parts and testing equipment, among others things very expensive, which in turn hampers the growth of the industry.

All in all, there is need to review most of the policies in place and ensure that they are conducive to good milk governance and the promotion of the dairy industry. Collaboration, co-ordination, harmonisation, implementation and enforcement of these policies will contribute to other efforts of developing the dairy industry in Ankole and the country at large.

Failure to compete effectively could largely explain why most milk processing factories that had opened for business in Mbarara immediately after the economy was liberalised, have gradually closed down. Their closure suggests that they failed to adjust to pressures of liberalisation that constantly require firms to be innovative and beat the odds in order to survive. Before examining the problems currently facing the milk industry in Ankole, the next section discusses the reasons for the failure of most processing factories in Mbarara.

The Rise and Fall of Milk Processing Factories in Mbarara

a) Unfavourable Loans and Interest Rates

One of the major setbacks, highlighted by former factories owners, was the dollar rated loans and the depreciation of the Uganda shilling. All factories established after liberalisation got loans in US dollars, with high interest rates of over 25 per cent. The loans were to be paid back in US dollars. However, the debtors were selling their milk products in Uganda shillings. Therefore, with the increasing depreciation of the Uganda shilling against the dollar, it proved increasingly difficult to repay the dollar loans.

The high interest rates attached to these loans also constituted a major hindrance to the success of these processing factories. Interest rates have on average ranged from 15 – 30 per cent for the period 1990 – 2000[52]. This negatively affected debtors' returns, ultimately rendering them bankrupt.

b) Acute Competition Amidst No Regulations

One of the major reasons given for the destruction of the market for processors is stiff competition from the vendors who sell unprocessed milk of dubious quality at very cheap prices. According to former factory owners interviewed, the poor regulatory framework within the country has been the principal cause of their business misfortunes. In Uganda, the set standards for the sale of raw, hygienic milk are not enforced and vendors continue to maximise profits by abusing the milk trade.

c) Lack of Government Support

The lack of government support to promote milk processing was also highlighted as a major problem. Although all these factories were initially given tax holidays for three years, the former factory owners claimed this was not enough, especially when compared to government support dairy industries get abroad[53]. Also, the increased importation of dairy products caused a major set back. Table 6.3 shows that even after establishment of these factories, Uganda's imports of milk and milk products increased from 1990 to 1997. This made it very difficult for processing factories in Mbarara to compete and as such many had to close down towards the end of the 1990s.

Table 6.3:Estimated Dairy Product Imports into Uganda[54]

Product description	Quantity imported			
Year	1990	1997	2000	2001
Milk powder	2,698,592 kg	3,756,235 kg	2,401,774 kg	1,285,120 kg
Milk powder specially Prepared for infants	33,486 kg	40,329 kg	11,702 kg	1,927,326 kg
Liquid milk (UHT)	2,431,388 lts	2,570,498 lts	1,006,852 kg	-
Condensed milk	53,927 kg	60,869 kg	46,835 kg	1,391 kg
Other milk and cream	80,155 kg	90,806 kg	136,572 kg	154,460 kg
Cheese	-	194,647 kg	216,854 kg	-
Ice cream	138,861 kg	167,987 kg	175,551 kg	91,608 kg
Yoghurt	1,780 kg	6,960 kg	8,406 kg	61,218 kg
Ghee, fats & oils	-	67, 000kg	32,027 kg	1,840 kg
Whey & modified whey	-	-	106,835 kg	32,370 kg
TOTAL	**5,438,189 kg**	**6,955,331 kg**	**4,143,408 kg**	**4,348,781 kg**

Source: Uganda Revenue Authority, 2003

It should be mentioned here that effective local demand for locally produced milk has remained very low because most middle class Ugandans tend of prefer to buy imported products as opposed to locally produced items. Some prefer exotic drinks instead and tend to think that locally produced goods like the UHT packs produced by factories in Mbarara are inferior[55]. This, according to the former factory owners, coupled with the continued importation of dairy products meant that the embryonic factories in Mbarara could not survive.

d) Lack of Market and an Aggressive Marketing Strategy

Most of the big processors were engaged in the production of similar products. They were either engaged in producing pasteurised milk or UHT milk. But as mentioned earlier, with the low consumption levels of milk domestically, the market had to be limited. Ugandans do not drink a lot of milk locally. The per capita consumption levels, as noted earlier, are as low as 30 litres per person, per year, which is certainly lower than the WHO recommended minimum average per capita milk consumption of 200 litres (*The Monitor*, 25 June 2003). There is no milk-drinking culture and neither the government nor the private companies did much to increase awareness amongst the population about the value of drinking milk. There were no aggressive marketing campaigns or advertisements compared to that of other beverages such as Coca Cola and beer. As such, Ugandans continued to provide only a limited milk mainly in the urban areas.

Only a few factories were able to expand into the regional market but due to problems of quality, transportation and distribution, these ventures were not sustainable. None of the local milk processors were ISO-certified or complied with any of the internationally recognised quality assurance certifications. As a result, foreign markets for Ugandan milk and milk products were limited. In this era of globalisation, the product penetration of foreign markets must meet the highest quality standards.

e) Lack of Qualified Technical Personnel

DDA officials claimed that a major cause of the closure of some of the factories in Mbarara was the employment of unskilled workers to man a highly technical industry. Dairy processing is by its nature a highly sensitive technical industry that needs well-qualified production and marketing managers as well as dairy technologists to run it effectively. According to one DDA official[56], most of these factories ran as family enterprises employing unqualified relatives or friends, which no doubt affected their performance. The fact that Uganda has no credible dairy training institute has meant that the factories had to hire technicians from abroad and this proved to be expensive for the firms. Ultimately the costs of production increased and this affected the growth of the sub-sector.

Evidently the milk industry in Ankole has been facing with a number of challenges, which need to be addressed in order to promote the further development of this sub-sector in this era of liberalisation. The previous milk companies in Mbarara were financially and managerially weak, physically and socially remote from the end markets and internally too inflexible to manage changes in production, in order to satisfy particular markets. That is why most of them closed down. This state of affairs in the milk processing industry in Ankole appears to bear out a well-known argument that globalisation in developing countries propels local industries to a "race to the bottom"[57]. Nevertheless, there is potential in the milk industry and attempts need to be made to eliminate the bottlenecks in the supply chain in order to promote the industry in Ankole. The next section looks at the bottlenecks along the milk supply chain in Ankole.

4

Major Bottlenecks Along the Supply Chain in Ankole

This chapter presents an analysis of the major problems affecting milk productivity, processing and marketing in Ankole and establishes obstacles to milk as an engine of growth and development in the region.

The Bottlenecks for a Farmer in Ankole

Milk production in Ankole, from the farmers' perspective, is faced with a number of problems which arise from a number of factors ranging from land management, cattle care, farm inputs, markets and the costs of drugs and veterinary services, to mention but a few. Some of these problems have been explained in the preceding sections as having been compounded by liberalisation and are justified by the following observations.

Low Farm Gate Prices

One of the major problems highlighted by all farmers in Ankole was that of low and fluctuating farm gate prices (see appendix 4). The lack of market and over supply of milk has meant that farm gate prices for milk have remained low and buyers dictate the prices for the individual farmers. All the milk buyers, whether processors or vendors, seem to be following a policy of pushing down farm gate prices of milk as many farmers complained of low prices and increasing milk rejections by both processors and vendors leading to massive losses for the farmers.

Other pressures identified relate to the requirement that a milk supplier ought to remain loyal to one milk vendor or else his/her milk will be rejected and this for most farmers is daunting. For farmers who supply processors, the issue of quality assurance is putting much pressure on their meagre resources considering that the income from the milk is not sufficient for undertaking effective farm management. Many have had to mobilise funds from other sources to invest in putting up milk sheds/parlours, for instance, to ensure hygiene and also improve pastures and are therefore producing at a loss.

Some farmers indicated that they supply the milk on credit and when the milk goes bad, as in the case of vendors, it is the producers who bare the loss as payment is often effected after the milk has been sold. Some vendors also request farmers to accept longer payment terms and at times just disappear without honouring their debt. Farmers especially in Nyabushozi who have been mostly prone to this kind of manipulation have now learnt whom to trust and deal with and whom not to trust.

The fluctuation of prices during the dry and rainy seasons compounds the problem, making it extremely difficult for a farmer to make any plans for development. During the rainy season when milk is plenty, farm-gate prices often hit the rock bottom. In the dry season, prices become better though farmers remain in a cycle of limited incomes.

The failure to improve farm management at the farm level due to low farmer incomes is a major hindrance to the flow of milk along the supply chain in Ankole.

Poor Management of the Farm Structures

Farming requires proper management. Most of the farmers visited did not manage their farms well, which they attributed to the lack of capital limited or lack of know-how.

Even on open grazing farms, there were huge bushes and as a result, cattle were prone to disease as these bushes harbour different types of vermin such as ticks and tsetse flies. These cause trypanosimiasis (locally known as *ekipumpuru*) and tick fever (locally known as amashuyo). The farmers here expressed ignorance of the fact that it would be better to reduce their herd and establish smaller better-managed farms. Most of the farmers in areas where open grazing is mostly practiced (such as Nyabushozi and Ntungamo), value the quantity of their herd as opposed to its quality and do not care much about improving their farms.

In Nyabushozi, particularly, more bushes have sprung up. According to many farmers interviewed, these bushes have come up as a result of the farmer's attempts to clear the symbopogan grass commonly known as "omutete." According to them, Nyabushozi as recently as the 1960s did not have the large bushes of today known as *Lantana Kamara*. These bushes seem to have expanded rapidly with more farmers settling in the area and trying to clear the area of omutete a non-cow paltable grass. As one farmer put it, that the farmers have had to uproot guarded against the sprouting of the thick bushes they are now battling with.

However, because of low prices, many farmers complained of the high costs of farm management today. The few paddocked farms show evidence of the need to repair fences with new poles as well as to clear overgrown shrubs.

Other features missing on the farms visited include milking parlours and calf pens. A milking parlour should contain feeding troughs for supplementary feeds such as banana peels which are normally fed to lactating cows during the milking time. The calf pens on the other hand, are often provided with a strong floor and clear drainage to avoid filth. Some of the young calves are provided with grass carpeting (okwarira) in their pens. In order to have all these structures in place, a significant investment is required.

The poor or non-existent farm management practices in much of Ankole has hindered the efficient flow of milk along the supply chain for milk especially due to quality problems. For the smooth flow of milk from the farm level, quality control and farm improvement must be advanced right from the feeding and care of the cattle.

Lack of Veterinary Services and Poor Mechanisms for Disease control

Good cattle-keeping requires regular veterinary attention as animals are susceptible to a number of diseases. As noted in Chapter four, the diseases affecting cattle in Ankole are plentiful, yet the services of the government veterinary doctors are very inadequate.

Currently, only one government veterinary doctor is posted at the sub-county level and judging from the number of cows committed to his care, this is insufficient. The alternative for most farmers has been to hire veterinary services from private veterinary doctors who are very costly and demand high fees. According to many farmers interviewed, their cattle go for long periods without treatment when suffering from certain diseases such as lung worms, intestinal worms, or even bilharzias, which they cannot easily detect until the disease has become very acute. This has affected milk productivity and quality.

With the onset of decentralisation, the sub-county veterinary doctor has also been given the task of planning for the sub-county, which means a huge work overload[58]. According to Dr Joshua Zimbe, a sub-country veterinary doctor, it is difficult for it is difficult for a veterinary doctor to single-handedly vet to provide clinical care for the animals in his area. He however noted that his terms of reference do not include providing clinical veterinary services. He explained that his assignment involves such activities as offering permits for transferring of animals, administering vaccines provided free by the government, monitoring the control of contagious diseases such as foot and mouth disease, inspecting the handling of milk by the buyers, educating farmers to stop using jerricans and training them in best practices for livestock keeping, milk hygiene and planning for the sub-county[59]. He further observed that treatment of sick animals is not the responsibility of government veterinary doctors. He however, pointed out that some veterinary doctors are able to assist farmers as whenever the need arises, usually at a fee.

It should be noted that the costs of maintaining a veterinary doctor at the rural level are very high and require the support of government. The local governments in many instances have failed to raise the counterpart funds to pay for logistics such as demonstration kits and transport even for undertaking the duties prescribed above at the county level and this has rendered many veterinary doctors ineffective. At the moment, the Uganda government does not pay for veterinary services to the farmers except for vaccinations and training offered at the sub-county level, though this is sometimes forthcoming.

The issue of training in particular is very problematic. According to the veterinary doctor for Kenshunga, conducting training workshops periodically is almost impossible as facilitation from the government is limited and irregular. He noted that veterinary services even under the decentralised system are under funded, often being allocated only 2% of the entire budget.

Due to the high veterinary costs, most farmers often do not utilise veterinary services and instead opt to treat the cattle themselves, yet they lack the skills for the proper treatment of the animals. The situation is made worse when a neighbour's herds carrying diseases enter into the farms and infest the cattle. A farmer at Bwizibwera in Kashari, Mr. Kasheka, expressed anger at people who often break into his cleared farm to feed their cows, steal his water and infest his farm with ticks and so cause his cattle to suffer from tick fever and other diseases. There are many such conflicts in other areas of Kashari, which often experience acute spells of drought in particular Nyabushozi. Farmers scramble for water and pastures in others farms especially during droughts and the dry seasons. Able farmers in such areas where the farm holdings are very huge have had to hire security personnel to keep away intruders during the dry season.

High cost of Drugs and their Poor administration

A major difficulty now faced by the farmers is the high cost of drugs for their animals. Drugs are expensive relative to the income earned from milk. As a result, farmers often find it hard to buy all the prescribed drugs for their cattle. Recommended drugs to be kept in stock by every farmer include *Penicillin, Ngombe-Mycine* and *Curamycine* (which are all injectables) and *Virmozalo,* (which is a drench drug), accaricides and those for tick fever, which is a common cattle disease in Ankole[60].

With liberalisation of the economy, drugs can now be bought from any drug shop. Since most of the farmers have no adequate training, their administration of drugs is doubtful in terms of measurements and correctness of dosage. The storage of the drugs is also poor. Some are kept for too long and expire. Yet farmers refuse to discard such expired drugs and use them to the detriment of their animals' health.

One of the farmers, Mr Bahikaine interviewed in Isingiro[61], *lamented that at times he administers under-doses knowingly because of the high cost of drugs. As he put it, "It is a question of economising regardless of whether they get cured or die, what else can one do?". He is aware this is not right but out of desperation, he administers drugs incorrectly.*

The drug issue is very challenging for farmers in Ankole. Many of the farmers interviewed lamented the increasing costs of drugs and the failure of the government to assist them especially in light of the declining prices milk. Mr Kabachenga of Biharwe Kashari for instance owns about 100 cattle[62]. He indicated that he needed four bottles of drench[63] called *Mebendazole* which costs approximately Ug sh 50,000 per bottle, for each drenching session. He therefore would need Ug sh 200,000 worth of drugs per quarter and Ug sh 800,000 for the whole year, to drench his cattle effectively[64]. Yet the same farmer only milked 20 cattle at the time of interview and he indicated that his average milk sales were 30 litres per day, at the price of sh. 200 shilling per litre. Mr. Kabachenga noted that the strain on his finances often forced him to sell some of his cattle so that he can afford the correct dose.

According to the district veterinary officer, Bushenyi, although ten years ago 40 litres of milk had to be sold to buy one litre of accaricides, today with increased liberalisation, about 600 litres of milk have to be sold to acquire a litre of accaricides and this shows the gravity of the situation.

Insufficient Government Assistance

Some farmers in Ankole indicated that they received no government assistance except for vaccination and guaranteed services for the prevention of diseases and control of contagious illnesses such as foot and mouth disease. This service however, is also not widespread as farmers lamented that their herd were never vaccinated.

In some areas, such as Nyabushozi, the government subsidized the construction of water dams. Farmers who could afford this were able to have a dam constructed on their farms at subsidised costs.

Some dams cost from two to Ug sh nine million depending on the size requested. Farmers only had to pay 50 per cent of the cost while the rest is borne by the government. However, those farmers who could not afford to pay remain desperate for assistance.

Several farmers interviewed during the field visits indicated that during the Obote I government (1962 – 1971), cattle farmers were better off, because they received subsidies on all purchases of drugs and the construction and maintenance of dip tanks and water dams, paddocking and tsetse control. Currently, however, under the liberalisation era, government gives very limited assistance if any.

The lack of Government assistance to farmers is creating a lot of concern and threatening farmers' in milk production. Many farmers talked to appealed for interested increased government co-operation such as subsidised farm implements like milk cans and drugs.

Lack of Capital and Limited Assistance from NGOs

Partially in response to the declining role of government, a number of NGOs have sprung up recently to assist farmers, but their impact on the ground is still negligible[65]. Of the 105 farmers visited in Ankole, only 33 per cent received NGO assistance in terms of training or donation of heifers. The majority 67 per cent, had never received any form of assistance (see Table 6.1).

Regarding loans acquisition, only 22 per cent of the farmers have accessed loans from banks and other financial institutions to improve their farms. Most of the farmers acquired these loans in the mid sixties when the government was encouraging them to look after hybrid cattle for commercial purposes. The loans were largely used for the purchase of hybrids as well as the construction of dip-tanks and fencing.

Table 4.1: Loan Acquisition and NGO Assistance

Loan Acquisition   /   NGO Assistance

County	Number of Respond-ents	Acquired Loan	%	Never Acquired Loan	%	Received Asst. from NGO	%	Never Received Asst. from NGO	%
Nyabushozi	15	6	40	9	60	4	27	11	73
Kashaari	15	3	20	12	80	4	27	11	73
Isingiro	15	0	-	15	100	0		15	100
Igara	15	5	33	10	67	8	53	7	47
Sheema	15	6	40	9	60	8	53	7	47
Rubaare	15	1	7	14	93	5	33	10	67
Ruhaama	15	1	7	14	93	6	40	9	60
Totals	105	22	21	83	79	35	33	70	67

In Nyabushozi, 40 per cent of the farmers indicated they were granted loans recently, mostly for clearing their farms[66]. Most of the farmers indicated that they used the money to make water dams on their farms. By contrast, Ruhaama and Rubaare counties registered the highest number of farmers who had never acquired loans (93 per cent) or received NGO assistance (67 & 60 per cent respectively) and this may well explain why milk productivity in Ntungamo is perhaps the lowest of these three districts.

None of the farmers interviewed in Isingiro county indicated they had received either bank loans or NGO assistance. This could be attributed to the fact that whereas in other areas there were farmers' organisations, in Isingiro only a limited number of farmers interviewed indicated they were members of any co-operative. According to an NGO official, the lack of farmers' co-operatives makes it difficult for NGOs to work there. He noted that they prefer to work with societies and not individuals. From my interview with Land 'O' Lakes one of the officials of the most common dairy-related NGO in Ankole,[67] Isingiro county has yet to be included in their programme area.

Water Problems

Ankole is a savanna area and gets rain seasonally, normally twice a year. The rain falls in March to May and September to December. These are the seasons when the milk is plentiful because the grass is plentiful and the wells full of water. During the dry season, however, which usually falls between June – August and Jan – March, the grass is scarce and there is no water in the wells. It is during these periods that the milk supply is low and the price is high. It is also during these times that there is a scramble for grass and water and the interference of some farmers into their neighbour's paddocks, creating conflicts as noted in sub-section 6.1.3.

In all parts of Ankole the impact of the day and rainy seasons is highly pronounced. My study reveals that there is a big variation in raw milk farm gate prices between the two extremes (rainy and dry seasons) with prices dropping to less than Ug sh 50 in some areas during the former while in the latter it goes up to Ug sh 350 or even Ug sh 400 per litre. In some areas, like Nyabushozi during the wet season, at times milk is left uncollected and wasted.

It was further observed that during the drought of June-October 1999, some farmers were forced to transfer their cattle from badly hit areas like Kashari to some areas where they could find more water and grass like Igara and Sheema. In so doing, the farmers have to look for friends with bigger farms where they can take refuge. This comes with a very high cost to both farmers as the in-coming animals interfere with the hosting farm, which is uncomfortable to both herds and often causes the rapid spread of infectious diseases.

In order for a cow to produce milk it needs to drink enough safe water. The lack of sufficient water in many parts of Ankole, particularly Nyabushozi, partly explains the lower levels of productivity compared to the other parts of Ankole, which rear indigenous cattle such as Kashari, as the climate here does not get so dry. Bushenyi, however, does not face this problem because its climate is much cooler.

The common way of getting water for cows in the drier parts of Ankole is through the digging of wells and water tanks. But these reserves lead to stagnant water. Wells and valley tanks keep water that is infected with bilharzia, a common cattle disease in Ankole damaging lungs and livers of cattle[68]. Consequently. many cows in Mbarara district especially, are sickly which affects the quality of milk[69].

In Nyabushozi, as noted above, farmers often have to move long distances in search of water because of the drier climatic conditions and seasonal droughts that dry up the available wells and dams. To prevent this movement, government has since 2000 been providing limited subsidies to individual farmers who can afford to construct valley tanks on their land, a practice that attracts envy from other cattle keepers in Ankole[70]. Earlier on too, in 1995, the government, thanks to a World Bank loan, provided assistance to Nyabushozi county in Mbarara district to have valley dams constructed for communal use[71]. This exercise however, led to massive corruption and mismanagement and up to today, some of these valley dams have never been completed. Some government officials were accused of embezzling the funds for this project but none have so far been brought to book. The issue of water scarcity particularly in Nyabushozi remains a burning issue, which was highlighted by many of the farmers as a key problem during this research. However, according to some farmers, the provision of communal dams is no longer a viable idea because farmers now have individual farms. Several farmers suggested that it would be better if government provided more subsidised loans to individual farmers, so that they can continue to construct their own individual dams on their farms.

Bush Burning and Environmental Degradation

The practice of bush burning, common in Ankole, leads to the destruction of cattle grass. During the dry season, people ignite bush fires causing havoc to the environment and depriving cattle of grass grazing. Some farmers believe that after burning the bushes, new grass which is succulent for the cows will germinate and give them more milk. This is especially common in the flat areas of Nyabushozi and Kashari. Other farmers, believe that burning bushes destroys ticks and tsetse flies. According to Mr Barigye, the district veterinary doctor for Mbarara district[72] however, such grass burning is a very negative practise and should be discouraged because it leads to the springing up of poorer pastures and the destruction of the soils.

Animal Security

Cattle theft has increased of late in parts of Ankole. According to the regional police commander Mbarara, the number of cattle cases reported in the district has increased from 2 per cent in 1990 to about 10 per cent in 2003. Cattle thieves come at night and steal cows from a paddock or kraal[73]. This is because cattle fetch high prices in Kampala where they are taken for slaughtering. Farmers have no protection for their animals at night. The animals are often left unguarded and their enclosures are not secure. Animals can therefore easily be led out of their night paddocks or enclosures with no resistance or fuss. In most cases, the stolen cattle are never recovered. If, however, they are recovered, the thieves end up being released or freed on payment of bribes due to flaws in our judicial system. Such thieves often repeat their game, leaving many farmers in Ankole insecure.

Increasing labour Costs and Problems of uncommitted workers

Many farmers interviewed in Ankole noted the problem of increasing labour costs. Maintaining a farm is an expensive undertaking as was observed on the farm of one Mr. Rugunda in Kashari. "The farm requires that there be a management composed of grazers, bush clearers, milkers and milk deliverers among others....," he said. My observations revealed that the labour costs mainly depended on the wealth of the farmer. For those on the top of the range with good model farms, the workers on the farm on average were paid Ug sh 50,000 per month, but such farms were few. The majority of the farmers visited indicated that the wages for labourers range from Ug sh 20,000/= to Ug sh 40,000 per month. In real terms, these are very modest wages as labour costs elsewhere in the country are much higher for casual workers.

Furthermore, most farmers interviewed expressed their disappointment at uncommitted labourers and cattle attendants who are often unfaithful. They indicated that labourers at times collaborate with thieves who steal their cows and that the cattle attendants do not graze the cattle to the owner's satisfaction. These hired labourers do not take pride in looking after the cattle and run away when they are faced with problems. Such workers make it difficult for the farmer to project for his farm.

Some of these cattle attendants also double as milk carriers (abacunda/abagyemuzi) and deliver milk to milk vendors or buyers. In this case, many end up diluting the milk to earn extra cash, but this spoils the reputation of the farmer. Because farm labourers are paid very low wages, most workers are not committed to their jobs, but this is also due to the fact that the farmer earns little from the milk. These management problems cause stress to farmers and creates disharmony on the farm. This ultimately impacts negatively on the animal care and eventually the farm and sector suffer.

Lack of Breeding Centres from where to Purchase Cattle

During the Obote I regime, when cross and exotic breeds were being introduced into Ankole, two animal breeding centers, at Nshara and Ruhengeri, were established for the provision of better quality cattle breed to farmers to promote milk production, at subsidised costs. Farmers purchased cows for stocking and bulls for reproduction of good quality cows for increased milk production. But during the Idi Amin's regime and subsequent governments, those centers were neglected and up to today there is no source in Uganda where good quality, milk-producing animals for restocking can be purchased. So the farmers are left at the mercy of unscrupulous business people who often sell them poor quality cows. Most farmers interviewed indicated that they purchased their cattle on the open market, which does not give them much choice for the selection of good stock/breeds for milk production. They suggested that they would prefer good quality bulls and heifers to be purchased by government and made available to them at a subsidised fee.

Lack of Supplementary Feeds

To obtain sufficient quantities of milk requires giving cows sufficient grass and water. However, in many parts of Ankole, particularly in Kashari and Nyabushozi, as indicated earlier, during certain seasons, grass fodder is scarce. In such periods, supplementary feeds are needed for cows to produce the sufficient milk. Supplementary feeds act as inducers to milk production but can only be purchased at a high cost[74].

Most of the farmers visited did not offer their cattle supplementary feeds because of high cost of the feeds and transportation. In farms situated close to urban centres, the most common form of supplementary feeds is banana peels, with a small sack going for Ug sh 700 on average, during the rainy season and Ug sh 1,500 in the dry season, in Mbarara town. An average cow would normally require a sack of peels as a supplementary feed per day, which goes to show how expensive even this type of feed is.

Lack of Training

A very important aspect of animal care is skills training for disease prevention and the proper methods of cattle care. Cattle treatment requires training for the farmers. Most of the farmers interviewed have not had such exposure and so caring for their farms poses a challenge for milk production especially because the cattle's health is not good. Such cases as worms, tick fever, tryponosomiasis and other cattle diseases affect cattle in many different ways and sick animals need proper handling. Lack of training renders farmers unable to care properly for their cows and to produce good quality milk. This accounts for the production of low literage and poor quality milk per lactating cow in many parts of Ankole.

Transportation problems and Poor distribution Networks

Three methods of transportation were indicated for transporting/delivering milk from the farm to the collecting centres. These include by pick-up/car, in containers carried on the head and by bicycle. The most common of these is bicycle transportation as 81 per cent of the farmers interviewed indicated they use bicycles to deliver their milk to collecting centres (Figure 6.1). However, none of the three methods is without risk/disadvantages. The car/vehicle may breakdown and on that day milk cannot be delivered. As regards the bicycle, it is likely to skid especially during the wet season and spill the milk. Finally, when it rains heavily no deliveries carried on the head are possible. All this indicates the risks and uncertainties within which farmers in Ankole have to operate and this puts them in a very vulnerable position.

In relation to transportation difficulties, there is the problem of containers used to transport this milk. Until recently, plastic jerricans were the commonest type of containers used by farmers to ferry milk to the collecting centres leading to the increased contamination of the milk.

Figure 4.1: **Mode of Transportation of Milk from Farm**

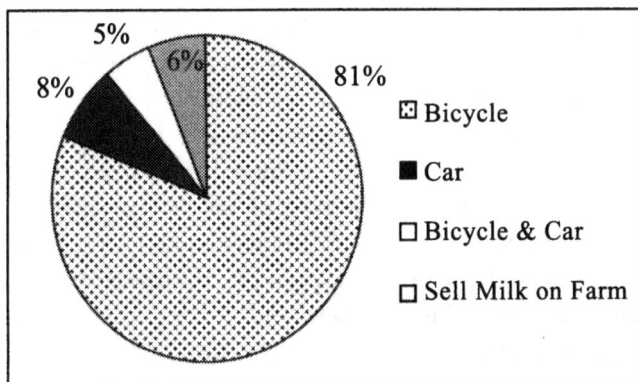

Source: Author's Fieldwork, March 2003.

Since the government ban on the use of jerricans in 2001, fewer are used nowadays yet there remains a need for the government and the regulatory body, DDA, in particular to enforce this ban more strictly as many farmers in the villages still use jerricans because they cannot afford the prices of the galvanised aluminium alloy milk cans. These farmers have appealed to government to provide some support services, to enable them to acquire cans.

On their part, milk buyers also indicated that transport problems are hurting their businesses especially when their vehicles break down. They appealed to government to provide them with subsidies to purchase refrigerated trucks. Only DCL has proper refrigerated vehicles and these are meant to ferry milk from the major collecting centres to Kampala where its processing plant is located. All the other milk vendors interviewed carried raw milk in cans on top of lorries, which spoils it quickly.

During the rainy season almost 50 per cent of the milk remains unsold in Ankole. This is largely because of inaccessible roads and as such prices paid to farmers can be as low as Ug sh 100 (US $ 0.05). As noted in chapter three, this has resulted in massive wastages of milk at the farm level when in fact other parts of the country are milk deficient[75].

Rejection of the milk by the Buyers

One of the major problems farmers face in Ankole is the frequent rejection of their milk. This rejection is caused by several factors emanating from the milk producers and milk buyers. In Nyabushozi, 53 per cent (the majority of the farmers) indicated they had had their milk rejected due to contamination. As noted in chapter three, this suggests that farm hygiene and handling of milk at the farm level in this area is poor (Table 4.2). Igara and Sheema had the lowest rejections of milk (2 per cent and 3 per cent) respectively, because of better farm management practices in this area, hence the better quality of milk.

Table 4.2: Rejection of Milk in Selected Areas of Ankole

County	Number of respondents	Farmers with milk rejected due to contamination	%	Farmers with milk rejected due to over supply	%	Farmers with milk not rejected at all	%
Reasons of Milk Rejections							
Nyabushozi	15	8	53	4	27	3	20
Kashari	15	6	40	6	40	3	20
Isingiro	15	4	27	5	33	6	40
Igara	15	2	13	5	33	8	54
Sheema	15	3	20	3	20	9	60
Rubaare	15	4	27	6	40	5	33
Ruhaama	15	5	33	4	27	6	40
Totals	105	32	30	33	32	40	38

Most of the milk buyers interviewed complained that milk producers sold them milk which is either diluted or one day old (*omurara*), or mixed the milk with corostrum (*omuhondo*) i.e milk from a cow which has calved within the last four days. In some cases it is the farmyard employees, who often dilute the milk, increasing the volumes sold in order to get surplus income for themselves.

Buyers also complained that milk is brought in dirty vessels/cans. As noted above, it is only until very recently that the Government banned the use of plastic containers as means of transporting milk by farmers and vendors. But some farmers still use them, because as noted above, the milk cans are too expensive to purchase. Because jerricans are very difficult to clean, milk put in such containers spoils fast and hence is often rejected.

In some cases the farmers' milk is contaminated as the result of milking a sick cow[76]. Such cows would have been recently injected or are on a course of treatment and would therefore be producing milk unfit for human consumption as, for example, when a cow is being treated in the teats when suffering from mastitis. Such a cow should not be milked but many farmers milk them, which affects the quality of milk.

Most farmers interviewed, however, complained that buyers conspire to reject milk especially during the rainy season. Farmers, particularly in Nyabushozi, indicated that buyers mix some chemicals in the milk and claim that it is bad if they have collected enough. Most farmers in Ankole indicated that this is a common practice during the wet season when there is a lot of milk[77].

Farmers also indicated that when one buyer rejects the milk, they sometimes take it to another buyer who accepts it. This leads them to conclude that the buyers are sometimes sincere when rejecting the milk.

Apart from direct rejection of the milk from the producers, the buyers have a habit of cheating farmers by not paying them regularly. Most of the times they buy on credit and when they have accumulated a lot of debt they change the locations of milk buying centers. This was noted to be most pronounced in parts of Kashari particularly where there was no indication of any farmers' organisation in place. This practice discourages farmers. Several of them indicated that they tend to switch from one milk vendor to another because of this problem, though they all tend to be exploitative. It is only DCL seems to generate some confidence among the farmers particularly for those close to its collecting centers, especially those that have organized themselves into farmers' associations or co-operatives. For such farmers, although the DCL payments are at times delayed, they do ultimately receive the money.

Most farmers interviewed indicated that they do not have any say in determining the price for milk and this makes them submissive to the buyers who dictate whatever price they want. However, as noted before, in areas where farmers have attempted to organise themselves into farmers groups or associations like BUDICO or ADAP, they have somewhat stabilised the prices for milk. It is therefore important that farmers organise themselves to have stronger bargaining power in setting better prices for milk. In the words of one very experienced cattle keeper in Ankole, Mzee Kabachenga in Biharwe sub-county of Kashari – Mbarara District[78]: *"A farmer can negotiate with the drug sellers the costs of drugs but he can't negotiate the price of his milk with the buyers."* This is the predicament for cattle farmers throughout Ankole.

The buyers also emphasized the erratic power supply which leads to loss of milk. Although all collecting stations with coolers have generators, there are times when these break down or lack fuel, leading to the closure of the centre and the subsequent rejection of the farmers' milk. Such instances however can largely be attributed to poor management at the collection centres.

Low Consumer Purchasing power

As indicated earlier, per capita milk consumption in Uganda is very low at 40 litres per person, per year. This can be seen in light of the fact that per capita income in Uganda is US $ 330 and 35 per cent of the population especially in the rural areas live on US $ 1 per day. This reduces the effective demand for milk. Income levels are no doubt a major determinant of consumption as households with higher incomes were observed to have higher per capita milk demand as opposed to the poorer households. In most low-income rural households visited during the research, expenditure such as school fees, lighting, clothing, salt, sugar etc were higher priorities than milk. Consumers who preferred processed milk were typically the sophisticated, health conscious, middle–income earners. They did not mind much about prices as long as the quality was good. Although many of my respondents mentioned taste as the reason for raw milk preference, price is the single most important determinant of this preference. In casual after-interview chats, many indicated they would like to consume safe, processed milk but just cannot afford it.

All these bottlenecks along the supply chain of milk as noted in chapters five and six have made it increasingly difficult for farmers to increase productivity and efficiency on the farm level, crippling the milk industry. The acute competition between different buyers has brought about confusion in the marketing of milk and unless a system of proper co-ordination between the production, processing and marketing nodes of the chain is developed, it will continue to be difficult to revive the milk sector in Ankole. The next section looks at the problems accruing to the milk buyers who deal in unprocessed milk.

Problems Accruing to the Milk Buyers / Milk Traders who deal in Unprocessed Milk

The dramatic increase in the number of informal milk traders[79] is a recent phenomenon prompted by the liberalisation of the milk sector in Uganda. This informal channel sells raw milk and undercuts the formal supply chain by selling it at low prices because they add no value to the milk, in most cases do not pay any taxes and do not bother with quality control. As mentioned before, this informal channel controls about 80 per cent of the market and as such the two existing processing factories in Ankole now operate at less than 50 per cent of their installed capacity.

Several problems were identified during my research relating to these buyers, which need to be highlighted as these have a negative impact on the smooth flow of milk from producers to consumers and have "informalised" the formal milk supply chain in Ankole. Such include the lack of temperature control, poor sanitation and adulteration all of which are discussed below.

Lack of Temperature Control

This refers to the failure of milk buyers/traders to retain milk under prescribed temperatures levels. As a result, they end up contaminating the milk in order to prevent it from spoiling. Milk traders run most collection centres without adequate equipment or technical skills for quality control and this constitutes a major obstacle for the milk industry in Ankole. Milk should be maintained at a temperature of 3^0C, which is the normal temperature of raw milk from a cow. However, right from the farm to the collecting centres, this is not adhered to.

Fresh milk needs to get to the consumers quickly but this is complicated by the fact that the distance involved in ferrying the milk from the farmers to the consumers is usually long – more than 400kms in the case of milk from Ankole to Kampala. So many customers end up with coagulated milk. In addition, because the milk is transported in unsuitable containers, often on open pick-up trucks and under high temperatures, it tends to spoil quickly. This is why most vendors end up contaminating it intentionally with hydrogen peroxide to try and stop it from coagulating.

Poor Sanitation

Several of the collecting centres visited had poor sanitation and used unhygienic containers. These adversely affect the quality of milk at this stage. Milk is a very delicate commodity and should be so treated. However, the manner in which it is handled at most of the collecting centres with dirty containers and unhygienic personnel spilling milk everywhere, leaves a lot to be desired.

Adulteration and Contamination of the Milk

Some farmers alleged that some traders add chemicals to the milk while testing it at the village level as many obviously do not mind about the quality of milk sold as long as they get their profits.

Some of the customers interviewed in both Mbarara and Kampala noted that at times the milk tastes rather different and that they often notice that it is adulterated but have no option and end up still buying it because it is all they can afford. According to Mr. Isha, quality control and monitoring officer, at DDA[80], many traders have in the past added hydrogen peroxide, sodium bicarbonate or potassium dichromate (starch) to increase the viscosity. He noted that most milk buyers and vendors add water as well which, in most cases is very dirty, to increase volumes and profits. He explained that tests carried on some samples by the DDA have found milk to contain residues of other chemicals like formalin, sodium carbonate and boric acid in order to make the milk look fresh appearance for several days after milking, traders illegally introduce these chemicals into the milk to arrest bacterial or viral growth and lower the acidity of milk.

Problems Accruing to Milk Processors

Liberalisation and technological progress have steadily altered the way in which milk processing is being undertaken in Ankole. Many processing factories in Mbarara as noted earlier now use imported technologies to process the milk in an effort to try and meet standards of quality that are set globally with regard to the export of milk. These UHT factories have to constantly ensure that they adapt to the best quality and most effective costs of production and engage in constant innovations, in order to attract business. This is especially true, in light of competing processing factories in other parts of the country and region.

Failure to compete effectively could largely explain why most processing factories that had opened for business in Mbarara immediately after the economy was liberalised have gradually closed down. Their closure suggests that they failed to adjust to pressures of globalisation and liberalisation that constantly require firms to be innovative and beat the odds in order to survive. Before examining the problems that current processing factories in Mbarara face, the next section discusses the reasons for the failure of most processing factories in Mbarara as described by the former owners and employees of these factories.

The Rise and Fall of Milk Processing Factories in Mbarara

Following the liberalisation of the Ugandan economy in 1992, several milk factories sprung up in Mbarara. However, today most of these have closed down and several reasons have been given to explain this failure.

Loans and High Interest Rates

One of the major setbacks highlighted by the former milk processing plants owners, was dollar rated loans and the depreciation of the Uganda shilling when the bulk of UHT milk products sales was in local currency. All factories established after the liberalisation of the enough acquired loans in US dollars, with high interest rates of over 25 per cent and had to payback the loans in dollars. However, with the increasing depreciation of the Uganda shilling against the dollar, it proved increasingly difficult. In 1994, for instance, the exchange rate between the Uganda shilling and the dollar was 1 dollar to Ug sh 979. In early 2003, however, the exchange rate was 1 dollar to Ug sh 2000[81]. The main complaint by all these factories was that banks could not consider the fact that their products were largely sold in local currency, which was continuously depreciating. So they ended up making financial loses and could not meet their loan repayment deadlines, ultimately closing down.

In addition, the high interest rates attached to these loans constituted a major hindrance to the success of these processing factories. Banks in Uganda have always charged the highest interest rates in the region, allegedly because the economy is not that productive. Considering that 50 per cent of Uganda's budget over the years has been funded by foreign loans and grants (despite 6 per cent GDP growth rate), it is no wonder therefore that domestic operations of the economy have been distorted. The Government through the Central Bank has been forced to increase bank rates continuously. These have on average ranged between 15 per cent – 30 per cent for the period 1990 – 2000,[82] and has discouraged borrowing. However, milk companies had no option but to import factory inputs such as packing materials and machinery parts, which required foreign exchange and this negatively affected their returns, ultimately rendering them bankrupt.

In most developing economies, such embryonic industries need to be protected and given subsidies for their initial take-offs if they are going to compete favourably in a liberalised world. Even in Western countries, fragile industries like the milk sector are highly protected and subsidised due to the highly competitive nature and vulnerability of the main actors in this sector.

Acute Competition Amidst No Regulations

Formal sector processors in Ankole were faced with acute competition from vendors and other processors in Kampala who were nearer the market, while the quality of milk from most farms in Ankole was and still is very poor.

One of the major reasons given for the destruction of the

market for processors is unfair competition with the vendors who sell very poor quality milk at very cheap prices, to unsuspecting customers. According to the former factory owners interviewed, the poor regulatory framework within the country resulted into such unfair competition. The processors add value to the milk during the processing process and this obviously makes their products more expensive than unprocessed products. In Uganda, the standards set for the sale of raw milk are not enforced and vendors who often want to maximise profits have abused the milk trade. As noted above (4.2.3), they adulterate the milk and add different unauthorised chemical substances to ensure that it does not get spoilt. They transport the milk to Kampala and sell it cheaply and the regulatory bodies have not done much to stop this. This practice is hurting the processing industry badly.

The main complaint of the current milk processors visited was of not having a level playing field with the vendors, which is killing their initiatives. They pleaded for government regulation to promote the sale of good quality milk, by for instance, banning the sell of raw milk unless it can be done through a well-managed cold chain. They also suggested that if every vendor was required to sell pasteurized milk, this would make it possible for them to break even and ensure the growth of the milk sector.

In addition, the poor quality of milk at the farm level was identified as another problem. According to Mr Musisi, the production manager of GBK[83], one needs very high quality milk to process UHT milk and this is very hard to get at a sustained level in Uganda today. As already indicated, this is largely because of poor hygiene at the farm level; cattle diseases, the none-existence of a cold chain from the farm to the factory; transportation difficulties of the milk from the farm to the factory due to lack of appropriate facilities and the poor road networks. Poor farm management and milking practices on the farm have aggravated the situation making the quality milk supplied by most farmers in Ankole very poor with exception of farmers in Bushenyi[84].

Over the years, there has been an in increase in the number of processing factories springing up in and around Kampala producing a variety of products from pasteurized milk to yoghurt, cheese, ice-cream and flavoured milk among others. These new factories consequently reduced the urban market for UHT milk processed by factories in Mbarara and this is why several of them had to close down. Since it is the urban population that has a higher propensity to buy such products as opposed to the rural population, all the processing factories were and still are targeting the urban market. Those located nearer Kampala therefore, had a comparative advantage over those in Mbarara.

Lack of Government Support

The lack of government support in promoting milk processing was also highlighted as a major problem (see also chapters 4 & 5). Although all these factories were given tax holidays for three years when they were being established, the former factory owners indicated that this was not enough especially when you compare the situation with other dairy industries abroad. The dairy industry in western countries, for instance, is most highly protected and subsidised[85] yet in Uganda, when the economy liberalized, these private investors had to tussle it out alone. The importation of diary products, for instance, kept on increasing even after the establishment of these factories. This no doubt affected the demand for locally processed milk. Table 4.3 shows that even after liberalisation, Uganda still depended much on imported milk and milk products as more imports were recorded from the period of 1990 to 1997 (see also next chapter). This made it very difficult for the processing factories in Mbarara to compete and many had to close down towards the end of the 1990s.

Table 4.3: Estimated Dairy Product Imports into Uganda[86]

Product Description	Quantity Imported			
Year	1990	1997	2000	2001
Milk Powder	2,698,592 kg	3,756,235 kg	2,401,774 kg	1,285,120 kg
Milk Powder Specially Prepared for Infants	33,486 kg	40,329 kg	11,702 kg	1,927,326 kg
Liquid Milk (UHT)	2,431,388 lts	2,570,498 lts	1,006,852 kg	-
Condensed Milk	53,927 kg	60,869 kg	46,835 kg	1,391 kg
Other Milk and Cream	80,155 kg	90,806 kg	136,572 kg	154,460 kg
Cheese	-	194,647 kg	216,854 kg	-
Ice Cream	138,861 kg	167,987 kg	175,551 kg	91,608 kg
Yoghurt	1,780 kg	6960 kg	8,406 kg	61,218 kg
Ghee, Fats & Oils	-	67, 000kg	32,027 kg	1,840 kg
Whey & Modified Whey	-	-	106,835 kg	32,370 kg
TOTAL	**5,438,189 kg**	**6,955,331 kg**	**4,143,408 kg**	**4,348,781 kg**

Source: Uganda Revenue Authority

In addition, the local demand for locally produced milk has remained very low because most middle class Ugandans have a tendency of preferring to buy imported products as opposed to locally produced ones. Some prefer exotic beverages instead and tend to think that locally produced goods like the UHT milk produced by factories in Mbarara are inferior. This, coupled with the continued importation of dairy products has meant that many factories could not find markets for their products in the country and thus could not survive. Under the liberalised economy, imported milk and milk products from other countries have also crippled the processing sector in Ankole. As revealed in Table 6.3, milk product imports have increasingly flowed into the country creating a stiff competition for the locally produced goods. The failure to protect these young embryonic factories therefore, contributed to their failure.

Lack of Market and an Aggressive Marketing Strategy
Most of the big processors were engaged in the production of similar products with limited variety. They were either engaged in producing pasteurized milk or UHT milk. But as seen earlier, with the low consumption of milk domestically, the market was limited and many

could not sell their products and hence made losses. Only a few were able to expand to the regional market but due to problems of quality, transportation and distribution, these ventures were not sustainable. In addition there were many barriers to milk exports as neighboring countries like Kenya realised that Ugandan products were beginning to hurt their domestic industries and introduced tariff barriers to protect their local dairy industries. This meant heavy losses for factories that had targeted the export market.

In addition, none of the local milk processors were ISO-certified (see chapter 5) and none complied with any of the internationally recognised quality assurance certifications. As a result, foreign markets for Uganda's milk and milk products was limited. In this era of globalisation, in order for goods to penetrate foreign markets they must meet the highest quality standards.

Ugandans do not to drink a lot of milk. The per capita consumption levels, as noted earlier, is as low as 30 litres per person, per year, which is certainly lower than the WHO recommended minimum average per capita milk consumption figure, which is at 200 litres per person per year[87], Ugadans do not drink much milk and neither the government nor the private companies did much to increase awareness about the nutritional value of drinking milk. There were no aggressive marketing campaigns or advertisements as for other beverages like soda and beer. Ugandans continued to provide only a small market locally for milk oftenly in the few urban areas. Household heads in the villages often prefer to spend their hard earned cash on the local brew alcoholic drinks or a beverages such as opposed to coca cola. The lack of effective local and regional demand therefore, affected the performance of these factories leading to their eventual close-down.

In addition, some of the former owners of the closed down factories did acknowledge that they had underestimated what was involved in the producing and marketing of milk in Ankole. For example, the need to have agents in each of the counties for proper milk collection and the need for aggressive advertising. It was established from the research that most entered into the business with hardly any experience in milk processing and marketing. Some also indicated that they had misunderstood important aspects of milk marketing assuming that they could easily achieve increases in profit margins. As Mr. Mahmood, a former employee of Ra-Milk Diaries, noted, " We entered into milk processing and marketing thinking that we could sell milk both locally and regionally on a competitive basis and had not realised how over-crowded the regional market was and the stiff competition existing in milk marketing"[88].

Currently the milk processors who are still in business have had to capture and retain specific milk suppliers in order to ensure a continued sale of good quality milk to specific outlets like supermarkets, hotels other and institutions. They are able to maintain a steady supply of raw milk by offering incentives to farmers that guarantee their loyalty on the input end of the chain (see chapter five), while they try to persistently improve quality to remain competitive and retain a share in the market on the output end of the chain.

Most of these processing firms, however, were more occupied with survival tactics and quick profits than with implementing long-term strategic decisions. On the marketing side, a former factory owner, for instance, confessed that when the going got tough, they would offer special concessions to supermarkets to take their milk and even offer more than three months credit and this no doubt impacted negatively on the organisation and performance of the individual factories[89].

Lack of Qualified Technical Personnel

One of the problems highlighted as a major cause for the closure of some of the factories in Mbarara is the employment of unskilled labour to man a highly technical industry. Dairy processing is by its nature a very sensitive industry that needs well-qualified production and marketing managers and dairy technologists to run it effectively. Most of the factories that closed down revealed that most of them ran as family enterprises employing unqualified relatives or friends, which no doubt affected their performance. The fact that Uganda has no credible dairy institute from which to recruit staff meant that the few technicians that were brought in were from abroad and this proved to be expensive for the firms. Ultimately, the costs of production increased and this affected the growth of the industry.

Evidently the milk industry in Ankole has faced a number of challenges, which need to be addressed in order to promote the further development of this sub-sector in this era of globalisation. The previous milk companies in Mbarara were financially and managerially weak, physically and socially remote from the end markets and internally too inflexible to manage changes in production lines to meet particular markets. This trend of affairs in the milk processing industry in Ankole appears to bear out a well-known argument about the consequences of globalisation for developing countries, namely that it can propel them into a "race to the bottom"[90]. Nevertheless, there is potential in the milk industry and attempts need to be made to mitigate the bottlenecks in the supply chains in order to promote the industry in Ankole. The next section highlights the problems facing existing processing plants in Mbarara according to the current owners and employees.

Major Problems facing the current milk processors in Ankole

The processors still in business in Mbarara face problems similar to those that their competitors faced, but specific challenges, were singled out however, as the most pressing problems facing the processing industry in Ankole today and these are highlighted below.

High Taxes

As noted earlier, taxes on imports are high and have been increasing as the government tries to improve its tax base. This has crippled the processing industry, which is heavily reliant on imports for spare parts, cleaning detergents and packaging materials. The production manager of Alpha Dairies indicated that even though they have been in business for a short while, they are already feeling the strain of high taxation. He explained that the taxes government levies including income tax (30 per cent), excise tax (10 per cent), property tax (4 per cent), withholding tax (5 per cent) and import tax (15 per cent) all take up over 50 per cent of the company's profits and this is hurting the factory. The operations manager of GBK on the other hand, noted that they have gone through a lot of hardship obtaining costly loans, which they are failing to pay back because they have to pay many taxes. This he asserted is suffocating their company.

Competition From the Vendors

As indicated earlier, processors face unfair competition from milk vendors who deal in raw, unprocessed milk and are not subject to any health or quality regulation. Because of their extremely low overheads and unethical practices such as dilution of milk with water, the latter can sell very poor quality milk at very low prices. Given that the majority of final consumers are price-sensitive, low-income Ugandans, the market share has now progressively been taken up by informal vendors and hawkers. The lack of regulation therefore, means that the informal milk trade continues to thrive at the expense of the formal milk trade which pays high taxes and incur heavy costs of production.

Inadequate Institutional Support

There is inadequate institutional support from government – this (includes line ministries and regulatory bodies) processing. Many of the policies are inappropriate and some have not been implemented or enforced. As noted in chapter five, the public health act for instance has not been implemented. Worse still, the penalties provided for wrong-doers (e.g a fine of $ 1 or imprisonment of not more than six months, for sale of unprocessed milk by unlicensed traders) are not a deterrent.

The regulatory bodies, due largely to the lack of funds, have not done much to implement and enforce the regulations relating to quality control, training and technical support to the processors in order to improve their businesses. This has impacted negatively on the processors.

As discussed in chapter five, the institutional constraints affecting the dairy industry in Ankole relate mainly to inadequate policies, out-dated laws and poor regulatory mechanisms.

Lack of Well Trained Dairy Technicians to man Milk Processing Operations

There are very few dairy technologists in the country and this has affected the performance of the dairy industry nation-wide, particularly the factories in Mbarara. The human resource requirements for the dairy industry in Uganda have not been met yet and the existing courses offered in some institutions such as Makerere and Bukalasa are not tailored to meet these needs. It was observed during my research that most of the employees of GBK and Alpha Dairies factories were not actually rained dairy technologists, but had been trained on the job to perform in an industry that requires highly skilled personnel to flourish.

In my interview with the quality control officer for DDA in Kampala, Mr. Isha noted that some of the processors do not appreciate the importance of hiring technical personnel and so these factories are not able to implement basic food quality management systems or good manufacturing practices, both of which are a pre-requisite for the production of good quality milk and effective sale of milk and other food products abroad. According to him, many mandatory tests are not performed due to lack of expertise at the factory, but according to the processors, dairy technicians are in short supply and it is costly for firms to hire them from abroad.

High cost of utilities

These factories incur high fuel and utility costs resulting in high operating costs. According to the production manager of GBK, they have very high costs for electricity and water. On average, GBK has been paying over sh. 15 million per month for electricity, yet at times the power is unreliable and some machinery has become spoilt due to this. The charges are equally unreasonably high for water and the processors wondered why the government cannot at least give them concessions on such utilities in order to promote their businesses.

Poor Marketing Strategies

Marketing strategies determine the levels of sales of any product. It was observed that this was lacking in the processors of Mbarara. None of them, for instance, were engaged in any aggressive advertising campaigns in contrast to competing beverages like coca cola and locally produced beers. Apart from a few advertisements on the local radio that are heard just once in six months, no other type of advertising was noted for the milk processors of Ankole.

Also the generation today does not want to become over weight so processors need to produce a variety of low-fat products like skimmed milk. The government ought to assist in advertising and promoting the milk consumption campaign especially in schools. In Kenya, for instance, the government used funds from the World Bank to sponsor a milk drinking campaign in schools for five years in the late 1980s and this led to a rejuvenation of the dairy industry. Today, Kenya, boasts of the most developed dairy industry in the region.

Increasing Imports of Milk products from Neighbouring countries and Abroad

Imports of dairy products from abroad and neighbouring countries which have active food legislation policy and more well developed dairy industries poses a big threat to the young and fragile processing industries in Ankole. Major supermarkets in Kampala and Mbarara have a variety of milk products from Kenya and South Africa on their shelves and many upper and middle class Ugandans tend to buy these products as they regard them of higher quality, than the locally produced products (see Table 4.3). This is frustrating local investors in the milk industry because they cannot quite compete with these products in terms of quality, yet.

Failure to Conform with International Quality Standards

Contemporary international trade requires that for any product to be sold on international market it must have an ISO 9000 quality management system. None of the milk processors in Mbarara have qualified for this. In addition, the current F.A.O milk quality standard to which every milk exporting country or company must adhere to stipulates high standards containing the following: low bacterial numbers (depending on the dairy product); the absence or very low numbers of potential human pathogens; zero tolerance for residues from veterinary drugs and minimal contamination from chemical and microbial toxins that may arise from feeds, treatment, pest control and the environment[91]. As processors in Mbarara do not yet adhere to these conditions, the market for their products is largely limited to within the country.

Lack of a Well-Managed and Efficient Cold Chain

Raw milk as noted earlier is highly perishable so it needs cold storage facilities right from the primary producer to the final consumer. Processors in Ankole however, lack efficient and effective cold storage capacity. Although Alpha Dairies has a few, processors in Ankole generally lack refrigerated trucks for milk collection and distribution and this has contributed to the high levels of milk spoilage.

Lack of Spare Parts

The lack of subsidiary offices representing machine manufacturers in Europe has meant that processors have to import spare parts from the country where the machinery was purchased and this has proved to be very expensive and has increased problems of servicing the machinery in time. As a result, some of the machinery ends up warring out faster than would be the case due to lack of regular repairs and maintenance. The production manager of GBK indicated that its production line for flavoured milk was only operational for a year and had to be halted due to the lack of spare parts.

Failure to Meet the Consumer Demands of the Local Population

The processing factories have failed to meet the various tastes and preferences of the customers as they tend to target only the high income, middle class consumers and this has limited their market. During my research, 50 milk consumers interviewed randomly in both Ankole and Kampala[92] to establish the preferences of consumers of processed milk versus raw milk, clearly stated that they preferred raw milk (75 per cent) as opposed to 25 per cent who preferred processed milk. This preference for raw (unprocessed) milk is an important factor in understanding market limitations[93].

For some customers, the characteristic flavour of fresh milk was lacking in processed milk and hence they prefer the latter. However, raw milk is cheaper than processed milk and although several respondents mentioned taste as their main reason for raw milk preference, price is the single most important determinant of this preference. To other consumers, however, the fact that vendors bring the milk to the door removes the hassle of having to travel long distances to buy it. Indeed, income levels determine the type of milk consumed as well as its frequency. Quite a number of respondents affirmed that, given an increase in their income levels, they would shift from raw to processed milk.

All in all, therefore, producers, traders and processors in Ankole still face a lot of challenges that need to be addressed if the milk industry in Ankole is to be revived, otherwise the remaining milk processors may also wind up soon. These key actors need to be enabled to produce sufficient milk, that is affordable of good quality, and can meet the different tastes and preferences of the population and markets beyond.

5

General Conclusions and Policy Recommendations

In this final section, I conclude by reflecting on the changes that the milk industry in Ankole has experienced following the liberalisation of the Ugandan economy. I also present some recommendations for the rejuvenation and future sustainability of the milk industry in Ankole.

Conclusions

Following liberalisation of the economy in the early 1990s, the milk supply chain in Ankole became more problematic especially after the involvement of the informal milk traders who deal in unprocessed milk. Although the milk industry in Ankole initially thrived under liberalisation, it has recently faced a lot of challenges including over-supply, low producer prices, lack of markets, quality problems and poor regulations. In particular, milk farm-gate prices in Ankole have been gradually falling over the recent past and this has frustrated milk producers. The competition from vendors has also made life difficult for the milk processors. As a result, the milk supply chain in Ankole is riddled with a lot of bottlenecks. Unless all stakeholders team up to eliminate these bottlenecks and establish well defined supply chains, the growth of the dairy industry in Ankole will remain a mirage.

In an increasingly globalised world, governments in developing countries, in collaboration with non-state actors need to support fragile and infant enterprises like the dairy industry in Ankole to survive. This calls for among other things, effective government regulation of the industry and the implementation of conducive policies that will promote and rejuvenate the sector.

A major conclusion from the study therefore, is that liberalisation per se is not conducive for the fragile milk industry in Ankole.

Although scholars such as Halit Yanikkaya (2003), have argued that open economies foster industrial development, the experience of the milk industry in Ankole seems to suggest the opposite. Unbridled competition coupled with the lack of regulation has hurt the milk industry. The lack of an effective regulatory mechanism in the era of liberalisation has increasingly led to limited profitability and hampered the growth of the industry[94].

After liberalisation, the dairy industry faced such as a small dairy market, weak processing sector and an aggressive informal sector. These problems need to be addressed in order to rejuvenate the industry. With the onset of liberalisation and the commercialisation of milk, the farmers in Ankole keeping hybrid cattle. Although the new breeds increased milk production, they also increased the costs of farm management. At the same time, the dismantling of co-operatives meant that farmers became more vulnerable to the market forces and exploitation by the milk buyers and processors. The initial upsurge of milk prices in the early 1990s thanks to liberalisation, has turned into a downward price spiral. The closure of processing factories in Mbarara has made a bad situation worse and exacerbated the farmers' frustrations. As a result, an increasing number of farmers are contemplating abandoning the keeping hybrid dairy cattle and reverting to the Ankole long-horned cattle. The findings of this study show that 30 per cent of the farmers have already acquired local bulls to cross-breed their dairy stock back to cattle for beef.

The present reality is that the future does not look promising for the key players in the milk industry in Ankole namely: that is the milk producer, the processors and the milk traders or vendors. On the contrary, unless urgent measures are instituted to increase farm productivity for good quality milk, improve the farm-gate price for milk and market and increase daily sales for processors, the future looks desperately bleak. At the same time, emphasis needs to be placed on increasing efficiency in the distribution of good quality milk on the part of vendors and improving product quality in general. The need for joint efforts in dairy development activities to cope with the challenges posed by the processes of liberalisation and globalisation is now more urgent than before.

In my opinion, a dairy development package, including all the parameters of clean, milk production along with processing, pricing policy and marketing infrastructure, is indispensable for the prosperity of the industry in Ankole. Short and medium term development projects such as small centralised processing units, clean milk production, the introduction of appropriate forage crops, milk processing by co-operatives, the improvement of animal health services, marketing infrastructure and other measures strengthen the dairy sub-sector must be acted upon by all stakeholders with the support of the government. The next section presents a summary of the main policy recommendations for the rejuvenation of the milk sub-sector in Ankole.

Recommendations

Dairying is reckoned to be an instrument of social and economic change (Gopalakrishnan & Lal, 2000). However, the many challenges facing farmers, traders and processors in this era of liberalisation have provided major obstacles in developing an economically oriented dairy enterprise in Ankole. The findings of this thesis have shown that the problems of the milk industry are multi-dimensional and interrelated. A long-term solution calls for practical involvement of the government in terms of 'new milk governance' and policy support. Stakeholders, associations, donors, farmers, and the private sector should combined their efforts to address the challenges facing this sector.

The Need to Provide Support Services

The development of a viable commercial dairy industry requires special support services in order to raise productivity and returns to smallholder dairying in Ankole. To engage in profitable and sustainable dairy production and marketing, farmers, vendors, milk traders and processors need to be assured of a stable milk market, technical support such as adaptive research, extension and breeding schemes, input supplies such as credit, and supportive policies relating to regulations, insurance and institution building. The free market, as an engine of growth for such a young and fragile industry, is a fallacy.

The development of the milk industry calls for state intervention and support.

Milk chains in Ankole involve both co-ordination and competition among all actors operating in the the sub-sector. The activities of these actors need to be streamlined and co-ordinated to rejuvenate the milk industry. All bottlenecks along the chain need to be addressed and removed. Farmers need to be sensitised about better dairy production systems and farm management practices for better yields in terms of quality and quantity. They need to be further trained in livestock management and provided credit to improve their farms. Milk vendors and traders also need to be sensitised about better milk handling and quality control. They need to be organised and to be given credit to improve their businesses. Milk processors should be given subsidies to increase productivity and incentives to stimulate the processing of milk and other milk products such as cheese, yoghurt, ghee, ice cream, etc. They also need assistance in accessing wider regional markets. One big investment possibility, which should be keenly explored, is the processing of excess milk into milkpowder.

The Need to Revive Cooperatives

Although co-operatives in Uganda were dismantled with the onset of liberalisation, they should be revived and strengthened to operate alongside private processors and milk vendors in the interest of small dairy farmers. Small milk producers cannot cope with the challenges of marketing a highly perishable product like milk single-handed. Co-operatives will not only hold the members' milk in own or rented coolers pending delivery to the processors, but are better placed to negotiate the terms and conditions of buying and selling milk than individual farmers.

Apart from marketing, co-operatives would assist in arranging for training. There is need to offer more training to farmers on how to manage commercially viable farms. Training programmes relating to quality control, better pastures and efficient farm management are very vital for the promotion of the milk industry in Ankole. The issue of the high cost of drugs also needs to be addressed. Again here, co-operatives can obtain such drugs and other farm inputs at negotiated bulk purchase rates and discounts.

There is need for some kind of subsidies to reduce the price of drugs and enable farmers produce better milk and look after their livestock better. Stronger cooperatives would also be responsible for providing farmers with veterinary services and sponsoring artificial insemination programmes. A dynamic dairy industry demands that producers and other stakeholders should constantly be updated on the prevailing market and investment opportunities in order to make informed decisions and choices. This can best be done through co-operatives.

The Need to Develop a Socio-Economic Model for Dairy Development based on India's "Anand Pattern"

The government needs to adopt a socio-economic model of dairy development for the milk industry in Ankole and indeed the country in this era of liberalisation. Several models exist but the "Anand pattern" adopted by the Indian Government could be the most appropriate (see Mbabazi's detailed PhD thesis [2004] - chapter 2). Among the key elements of the "Anand pattern" were of the creation of farmers' co-operatives at the village level as well as farmer unions and metropolitan dairies in the different states of India all of which co-ordinate the production, processing and marketing of milk. As a result, India today has one of the strongest dairy industries in the developing world. Uganda could learn much from India's experience, replicating the positive aspects of the "Anand pattern" in Ankole.

To achieve efficiency in milk collection and marketing, farmers elsewhere in Ankole need to organise themselves into strong village level co-operatives as their colleagues in Bushenyi district have done[95]. Through the use of self-regulating mechanisms, members would maintain milk standards right from the farm level. These village co-operatives would be charged with the collection of milk from the farms. They could then chill their milk and reduce on wastage especially during the wet season when milk is plentiful and the vendors and processors do not buy all the milk. From these village level co-operatives, co-operative unions should be formed to process the milk. By replicating the Indian "Anand Pattern" of village level cooperatives and processing unions, the milk industry in Ankole would no doubt be rejuvenated. These unions would provide market outlets for the farmers' milk, supplied by the village cooperatives at fair prices. Rural farmers would be freed from the exploitative middleman and urban consumers would get hygienic and nutritious milk. Furthermore, these farmers' unions could engage in the production of milk by-products such as cheese, yoghurt and ghee, offering consumers a variety of hygienic products and providing a bigger market for the farmers.

The Need to Diversify Packaging and Products for Processing Industries

Milk processors in Ankole should strive to satisfy different consumer tastes and preferences at affordable prices[96]. Milk packaging should be verified to suit different markets and customers' purchasing power. For instance, UHT tetra packs could be produced for the high-income and middle class Ugandans as well as for export, while other types of cheaper packaging can be devised for the local mass market.

Processors also need to diversify their final product outputs. Most processors have been concentrating on the production of UHT milk, which the majority of the local population cannot afford. More value-added dairy products like powdered milk, baby formulas, cheese, ice-cream, butter and yoghurt, which at the moment are mainly imported, can be produced on a larger scale to satisfy the demand. The production of these products would not only use up excess milk and to some extent pre-long its shelf life, but would also enhance export prospects and earn and save foreign exchange. Processors should therefore, be given incentives to go into the processing of these products.

The Need for Effective Policy Formulation to ensure Proper standards and Effective regulation

Effective policies need to be formulated and implemented in order to promote the milk industry in Ankole. An efficient supply chain for any commodity requires focused management policies. Mandatory regulations should be devised to ensure high quality milk from the farm level to the consumer and to minimise losses and wastage. Support services and mechanisms should be put into place to facilitate the production of milk products of the highest quality. The ministry of Agriculture, Animal Industries and Fisheries, local government other regulatory bodies should establish, implement and sustain the highest possible standards to effectively promote the dairy industry not only in Ankole but nationwide. The government and regulatory bodies should have realised by now, that today's laissez-faire situation cannot guarantee quality assurance and effective management along the milk supply chain[97].

The Need to Educate the Population about the Value of Drinking Good Quality Milk

All principal actors in the dairy industry should pay serious attention to the boosting of local consumption levels through sensitisation, advertisements, launching school milk drinking campaigns and increasing the purchasing power of milk consumers. Consumers need to be educated about the benefits of drinking high quality wholesome milk, free from harmful micro-organisms or any form of adulteration. One way of increasing the milk consumption in Uganda is to launch a school milk campaign, like was done in Kenya[98]. The government should provide money to give school children milk free of charge or at subsidised rates not only for nutritional purposes, but to boost the demand for milk for the benefit of the dairy industry.

Uganda could also learn lessons from other countries like the USA that have implemented such milk campaigns. In the face of decades of declining per-capita consumption in the United States, milk producers and processors banded together and launched an advertising campaign to raise awareness about the numerous benefits of milk consumption. This campaign, launched in 1994, utilised the simple slogan: "GOT MILK?" and employed celebrities to tout its health benefits. By 1996 "GOT MILK?" had achieved a 91 per cent awareness rating in the American public and is now recognised as one of the ten most successful advertising campaigns in history[99]. More importantly, the success of "GOT MILK?" is partially credited with stabilising and reversing the decline in milk consumption in the USA. The success of such a simple awareness programme in a market with as many substitutes for milk as the United States provides ample evidence that a similar campaign could be successful in Uganda.

The Need to Develop a Code of practice for the Production, Processing and Marketing of milk in order to assist Product Certification

Although Uganda's economy seems to be doing the right things, especially in terms of the 'Plan for the Modernisation of Agriculture' (PMA) and the numerous strategies put in place to expand exports, there is still much to be done for the milk industry. With a highly competitive market, Ankole milk needs to meet the highest quality standards, especially if the export market is to be targeted. Hence, there is need for the private sector and the farmer's organisations, with the support of government, to revise their strategies and find ways of producing the highest quality milk and milk products, to qualify for certification based on international standards. The milk processors in particular, need to be assisted to get their products certified to enable them target to the export markets[100].

A code of practice for milk production, handling, processing and distribution needs to be developed. This code should be geared towards having Ugandan milk producers, processors and traders conform to the Hazard Analysis Critical Control Points (HACCP) and International Standards Organisation Certification (ISO). The major food safety criteria for milk and milk products worldwide on which these standards are based include low bacterial numbers, the absence or minimum numbers of potential human pathogens, avoidance of residues from veterinary drugs, minimal contamination from chemical and microbial toxins arising from feeds treatment and pest control, to mention but a few.

The Need for Government and NGOs to Assist in Opening more Marketing Opportunities for Uganda's Milk and Milk Products within the Region

The government and NGOs should assist milk processors to devise an aggressive marketing strategy to penetrate the milk market outside Uganda, especially in the neighbouring countries where the demand for milk is still substantial. The milk processors should take advantage of Uganda's membership to the East African Customers Union and COMESA to aggressively market and export their milk products[101].

The ability of Uganda's dairy sector to take advantage of these opportunities will depend on its success in alleviating the bottlenecks, which currently impair its performance. As noted earlier, the government needs to give processors a big push. In South Asia, for instance, when the Coca-Cola company found initial difficulty in penetrating the market, the American Government did not lie back and leave the company to struggle on its own. It stepped in and negotiated deals so that today the whole of Asia is awash with Coca – Cola products. Similarly, the flooding of the American market by Toyota products required the Japanese Government to first negotiate a trade deal[102]. The government therefore, needs to be involved in opening export market avenues for Ankole – and Ugandan milk processors, so as to revive and develop further the dairy processing industry in Uganda. Milk processors should also work alongside the Uganda Export Promotion Board (UEPB) and the Uganda National Chamber of Commerce (UNCC) to actively identify and enter export markets in the Great Lakes region and beyond.

The Need to Protect Local Processors by Imposing High Taxes on Imported Milk and Milk products

Great potential exists for developing the local and export market for Ankole's dairy industry. However, most processors have failed to break-even due to the high competition from imported milk and milk products. For vulnerable industries like milk processing, government should offer protection until they are strong enough to stand on their own. In most Western countries, the dairy industry is one of the most highly subsidised and protected industries. The WTO rules allow for infant industry protection for selected sectors over specific periods of time and this is what should be done for the milk processing industry in Ankole. Imports of milk and other milk products from other countries should be highly taxed for a specified period of time until our embryonic processing industry has reached that critical stage when it can compete favourably. The government still has an important role to play in the rejuvenation of the vulnerable dairy industry sector.

The Need to Encourage and Support further NGO Involvement in the Milk Industry

The research indicated that there are a number of non-government and community-based organisations and institutions currently involved in the dairy sub-sector development in Uganda. Land 'O' Lakes, for example, has made efforts to do this through holding stakeholders seminars / forums and some limited success is being registered. Government needs to support and strengthen such initiatives.

Government's attempts to privatise the clinical aspect of veterinary services have not been successful and this has proved problematic and costly to the farmers. Government should enlist the involvement of NGOs in exploring alternative ways and means of providing veterinary services to farmers at affordable prices. More research to explore better options is recommended.

The Need to Develop and Improve Dairy-Related Institutions and infrastructure

There is need to build institutions and infrastructures, which can help promote the dairy industry and one key area is training and manpower development. Graduate engineers from most of our institutions of higher learning cannot even turn a motor or perform a simple milk test on milk[103]. According to the production manager GBK, dairy industry related training programmes should be launched to provide dairy technicians. DDA can work with institutions such as the Departments of Agriculture, Veterinary, Agriculture Food Science Technology University and Engineering at Makerere and the Agricultural College in Bukalasa to train the required technicians. Also, the milk collection infrastructure needs to be improved especially in the remote milk producing locations.

In addition, not a single farmer in Ankole uses machinery to milk cows. To ensure an improvement of the milk quality from Ankole, the government and NGOs should explore the possibility of supporting large-scale diary farmers producing substantial quantities of milk to install milking machines on their farms to improve hygiene and the quality of milk, save time and reduce labour costs.

The Need to Promote Traditional Processing

Traditional milk products such as cow ghee and yoghurt (*amakamo*) also ought to be promoted to supplement farmers' income from raw milk sales. Besides providing cash income cow ghee can be preserved for a rainy day or exchanged for food from neighbouring agricultural communities, especially during the dry season when milk is in short supply. Ghee is also a handy source of income for the wives of farmers who have no direct control over the spending of the milk money. Women use ghee money to meet their domestic needs which their husbands may ignore or not consider important.

Encouraging the traditional processing sector would undoubtedly reduce the spoilage of milk whenever for one reason or another. Such milk is not sold. Where there is excess supply, for example, milk should be processed into products with a longer shelf life than fresh milk. From an economic point of view, making more traditional Ankole dairy products for the local market which are of good quality would to some extent add value to milk and enable farmers not only to earn more money, but also to diversify their diary products. Locally produced products would be affordable to the peasant farmers who do not own cattle. The government should therefore, explore the possibility of making small appropriate technology processing units available to households for processing milk. The establishment of dairy products processing enterprises would create rural employment opportunities and reduce rural migration pressures. The potential for commercialising and expanding traditional milk processing should also be subject to further research.

The Need to Provide Farmers, Traders and Processors access to micro-finance and low interest loans

The issue of finance is very crucial and needs to be emphasised. The government should promote micro-finance institutions that can provide funding for this sector. Access to credit for farmers is almost non-existent and this has diminished the farmer's abilities to improve their farms or intensify their farming practices. Many farmers stressed the importance of credit facilities for dairy farming. The limited amount of finance that exists in the dairy industry seems to be concentrated just on the top of the chain. Milk processors are more likely to get loans and government assistance than farmers at the lower end of the chain. But even the processors complained that they do not have enough access to credit facilities. The lack of access to banks and other financial institutions in Uganda have been a major impediment to the progress of the dairy industry in Ankole.

The revival of co-operatives should hopefully provide a solution to the problem of lack of credit access for farmers and smaller milk traders. Co-operatives can easily mobilise funds and generate loans for members, which can be recovered from the milk sales. Big processors also need to access low interest loans to improve and expand their businesses. The government should step in and possibly through NGOs and donors, enable each of these key actors to access low interest loans in order to boost the milk industry in Ankole.

Integration of the Vendors / Informal Milk Traders into the Regulated Market Environment

Apart from improving the regulation of the industry, the government, should assist milk processors and vendors to explore other innovative distribution channels for fresh milk from Ankole. Milk vendors should be integrated in the formal milk market to curtail the supply of poor quality milk. Long-standing attempts in Kenya to suppress milk vendors have not been successful and therefore, the Uganda government should not assume that the regulation of the informal sector will be easy. It is however, worth trying.

The informal sector needs to be streamlined through the integration of hawkers into the regulated market environment. This would be in their own interests for it would grant them formal recognition and to benefit from whatever assistance is given to the dairy industry in future. More research should be carried to find out how the vending sector can be improved to create more jobs. Various strategies, including the organisation of the hawkers, the registration of their operations, training and sensitisation on milk quality and standards, the adoption of appropriate technology for milk pasteurisation, the use of appropriate equipment for transportation and handling to modernise the dairy industry should be implemented. Further research into this area is also highly recommended.

The Need for Further Research and Debate on the Usefulness of Supply Chain Analysis in Understanding the dynamics of locally traded goods such as milk.

In light of the limitations of supply chain analysis as a methodological tool for understanding the dynamics of locally traded commodities such as milk, it is recommended that further research is undertaken into the historical development of trade networks for other locally traded commodities like beans or maize in order to establish the different kinds of chains that exist and how these can be further supported and streamlined (See Nadvi Khalid 2004, on Chains for Pro-poor Development).

The debates and discussions about the production, processing and marketing dynamics of the milk industry in Ankole presented in this study suggest that supply chain analysts have not yet formulated a coherent theoretical framework with satisfactory explanatory power. Further debate is needed on clarifying key concepts (e.g. formal vs informal chains) and the historical dynamics of such supply chains. Efforts should be made to integrate the issues of regulation and standards in supply chain studies (see Messner 2002, and Ponte 2002, for attempts in this direction). Finally, there is need for better understanding of the conditions under which certain forms of governance emerge and their consequences, both in theoretical and policy-oriented terms (Nadvi, 2004).

To conclude this thesis report, it should be noted that although the milk industry in Ankole is still localised, it does have the potential for not only improving milk supply locally but also for developing an export industry within the region. The key element, therefore, is to identify a strategy through which raw milk can be sourced, processed and marketed in order to maximise profits. It is imperative that a system's approach to offering support for stakeholders and key players in the dairy sector be developed a process in which government must take the lead initiative.

References

Ankole-Watusi Cattle (2003), Breeds of Livestock http://www.ansi.okstate.edu/breeds/cattle/ankolewa/index.htm(Accessed May 2001).

Bamunoba, Y.K. (1973) "The Cult of Spirits in Ankole (Western Uganda)" Unpublished MA thesis, Makerere University.

Barrientos, S., C. Dolan and A. Tallontire (2001), 'Gender and Ethical Trade: A Mapping of the Issues in African Horticulture', *NRI Report No. 2624*. Chatham Maritime: Natural Resource Institute.

Bariyo, Rogers (1999), "Structural Adjustment Programmes (SAPs) in Uganda", Unpublished Seminar Paper, MUST.

Bank of Uganda (1986), "Annual Report" 1985, Kampala

Bank of Uganda (1999), "Monthly Economic Report" Jan-March, Kampala.

Bank of Uganda (various years), "Quarterly Bulletin of Statistics," Kampala.

Bigsten, Arne & Steve Kayizzi-Mugerwa (2001), "Is Uganda an Emerging Economy?" A Report of the OECD Project "Emerging Africa" Nordiska Afrikainstitutet, Uppsala. Research Report No.118.

Bornstein Ban (1999), "Milk Value: Got Milk Article 2," http://wwwmilk.com/value/innovator-spring99.html (Accessed March 2004).

Brett, E.A. et al (eds) (1997), *Uganda: Landmarks in Rebuilding a Nation* Kampala, Fountain Publishers

Chalimbaud, Julien (2001), "Mbarara Milk Project" Workshop Proceedings unpublished, SUMPCA.

Clancy, M. (1998), "Commodity Chains, Services and Development: Theory and Preliminary Evidence from the Tourism Industry," *Review of International Political Economy*, Vol. 5, No. 1 pp 122-148.

Collier, Paul (1994), *Economic Aspects of the Ugandan Transition to Peace*

J. P. D. Azam, P. Bevan, P. Collier, S Dercon and J.W. Gunning (1994), *Some Economic Consequences of the Transition from Civil War to Peace* CSAE, Oxford University.

Collier, Paul (1997), *Ugandan Trade Policy: Liberalisation in an environment of limited Credibility"* CSAE, Oxford University.

Cowan L.G. (1990), *Privatisation in the Developing World*, Praeger Publishers, New York.

Daviron, B. and P. Gibbon (2002), "Global Commodity Chains and African Export Crop Agriculture, Journal of Agrarian Change" 2(2): 137-161.

DDA (2002), "Annual Report 2001/2002", Kampala.

Doornbos, Martin (2000), *Institutionalizing Development Policies & Resource Strategies* in Eastern Africa & India London, Macmillan.

Faculty of Medicine, Mbarara University (2002), "Nutrition Baseline Survey, Selected Districts of Uganda, Mbarara."

Falvey Lindsay & Charan Chantalakhana (eds) (1999), *Small Holder Dairying in the Tropics,* ILRI (International Livestock Research Institute), Nairobi (http://www.cgiar.org/ilri/dbtw-wpd/fulldocs/smhdairy/smhdairy.htm)

(Accessed March 2001)

Gayle Dennis and Jonathan Goodrich (1990), *Privatisation and Deregulation in Global Perspective,* Princeton, Princeton University Press.

Gerrefi, G., D. Spener & J. Blair (eds) (2002), "The Governance of Global Value Chains: An Analytical Framework" paper presented at the Bellagio Conference on Global Value Chains, April 10-12.

Gerrefi, Gary and Miguel Korzeniewicz (eds) (1994), *Commodity Chains and Global Capitalism*, Westport CT, Praeger Publishers.

Gibbon, P. (2002), "South African and the Global Commodity Chain for Clothing: Export"Performance and Constraints CDR Working Paper 02.7." Copenhagen: Centre for Development Research.

Gibbon, Peter (2000), "Global Commodity Chains and Economic Upgrading in Less Developed Countries" February. Centre for Development Research, Copenhagen. CDR Working Paper 00.2.

Ghosh Jayati (1999), "Openness, Deficits and Lack of Development", in Martin Khor (ed) *Rethinking Industrialisation & Reshaping WTO,* Third World Network.

Gopalakrishnan C.A & Lal G.M.M. (2000), *Livestock and Poultry Enterprises for Rural Development,* New Delhi: Vikas Publishing House.

Handfield, R. B and E. L. Nichols Jr. (1999), *Introduction to Supply Chain Management,* New Jersey, Prentice Hall.

Hansen, Holger Bernt and Michael Twaddle (eds) (1988), *Uganda Now: Between Decay and development,* Oxford, James Currey.

Hansen Holger Bernt and Michael Twaddle (eds) (1991), *Changing Uganda. The Dilemmas of Structural and Revolutionary Change,* Oxford, James Currey.

Hansen, Holger Bernt and Michael Twaddle (eds) (1998) *Developing Uganda,* Oxford, James Currey.

Hoogvelt, Ankie (1997), *Globalisation and the Post-Colonial World; A New Political Economy of Development,* London, Macmillan.

IDS Bulletin (July 2001), "The Value of Value Chains; Spreading the Gains from Globalisation," Vol. 33 No.3, IDS Publications, Sussex.

Kaplinsky Raphael and Mike Morris (2001), "A Handbook for Value Chain Analysis" (Ottawa:IDRC)http://www.ids.ac.uk/ids/global/pdfs/vchNov01.pdf (Accessed March 2002).

Kasfir, Nelson (1994), "Strategies of Accumulation and Civil Society in Bushenyi, Uganda: How Dairy Farmers Responded to a Weakened State" in John Harbeson, Donald   Rothchild & Naomi Chazan (eds), *Civil Society and the State in Africa,* Boulder Lynne Rienner.

Katate, A. G. & L. Kamugungunu (1955), *Abagabe b'Ankole: Ekitabo 1,* Kampala, EALB.

Katz S. Bernard & Ahene A. Rexford (1992), *Privatisation and Investment in Sub-Saharan Africa,* Praeger, Wesport, New York, Connecticut, London.

Kisamba-Mugerwa, W. (1998), "Individualisation of communal Grazing Land in Uganda: An Overview of Basongora Land of Kasese District," in Clark Gibson et al (eds), *Common Property Resources Management in East Africa,* Kampala, MISR.

Land O' Lakes Inc (2000), "Report on the Milk Production and Market Chain Study," Kampala. Unpublished.

Land O' Lakes Inc International Development (2001a), "Uganda Dairy Business Development project" Kampala. Unpublished.

Land O' Lakes Inc International Development (2001b), "Report on Dairy Sector, Supply Demand and Competitiveness Study" (Final Report).

Land O' Lakes Inc International Development (2003), Export Handbook.

Marsden, T., J. Banks and G. Bristow (2000), *Food Supply Chain Approaches: Exploring Their Role in Rural Development, Sociologia Ruralis 41(4): 424-438.*

Mbabazi Pamela (2004), "Supply Chains and Liberalisation; The Milk Industry in Ankole." A PhD Dissertation submitted to Mbarara University, March 2004.

Mbabazi, Pamela & Timothy M. Shaw (2000) 'NGOs & Peace-building in the Great Lakes Region of Africa: States, Civil Societies & Companies in the New Millennium' in David Lewis & Tina Wallace (eds.) *New Roles & Relevance: Development NGOs and the Challenges of Change,* West Hartford, Kumarian.

Mbabazi, Pamela et al (2002), "Governance for Reconstruction in Africa: Challenges for Policy Communities and Coalitions", in *Global Networks: A Journal of Transnational Affairs* Vol. 2 , No.1, January. Oxford, Blackwell Publishers.

Mbabazi, Pamela & Rogers Bariyo (2003), "Globalisation and the Milk Industry in Uganda:The Case of Mbarara District,"_Unpublished paper presented at an International Conference on the Challenges of Globalisation and Pastoralism in Uganda, organized by Faculty of Development Studies – MUST at Rwizi Arch Hotel, Mbarara 4 – 6 February.

Mbarara District Brochure (2000), "Basic Development Indicators."

Michalopolous, C. (2001), Developing countries in the WTO_London, Palgrave.

Ministry of Agriculture, Animal, Industry and Fisheries (MAAIF) (2000), "The Plan for Modernising Agriculture - Eradicating Poverty in Uganda," *Government Strategy and Operational Framework,* Kampala.

Ministry of Finance, Planning & Economic Development (Various Years): "Background to the Budget and Statistical Abstracts," Kampala, (Various Issues).

Ministry of Health (2003), "Nutrition and Early Childhood Project;" An Evaluation Report, Kampala.

Mugisha, Odrek Rwabwoogo (1998), *Uganda Districts Information Handbook,* Kampala, Fountain Publishers.

Museveni, Yoweri K (1997), *Sowing the Mustard Seed : The Struggle for Freedom and Peace in Uganda,* London, Macmillan.

Museveni Yoweri K. (2001), "Socio-economic Indicators and Industrial Production to Measure Progress since 1986", Kampala, NRM Secretariat.

Mutibwa, (1992), *Uganda Since Independence: A Story of Unfulfilled Hopes,* London, Hurst & Company.

Nadvi Khalid (2004), "Globalization & Poverty: How can Global value Chain Research Inform the Policy Debate?" IDS Bulletin 35(1), January.

NRM Secretariat: (2001), "Consolidating the Achievements of the Movement, 2001 Election Manifesto, Kampala."

Ponte Stefano & Gibbon Peter (2004), *Trading Down? Africa, Value Chains and the Global Economy,* Danish Institute for International Studies, Copenhagen.

Rabach E. and E.M. Kim (1994), "Where is the Chain in Commodity Chains? The Service Sector Nexus" in G. Gerrefi and M. Korzeniewicz (eds), **Commodity Chains and Global Capitalism**, Westport: Greenwood Press.

Robertson R. (1992), *Globalisation:* London, Sage.

RELMA (2002), "Proceedings of a Regional Workshop on Milk Marketing," Mombasa Kenya, Whitesands Hotel.

Saammanya, J.P. (2002), 'Overview of the National Dairy Policies Reform Process and its Effect on Milk and Milk Products Supply and Demand in Uganda,' in "Proceedings of the Regional Workshop on Milk Marketing: From Producers to Consumers: Processes for Policy, Legal and Institutional Change in Milk Marketing," sponsored by RELMA, Whitesands Hotel, Mombasa Nov 25-28.

Sen, Amartya (1999), "Assessing Human Development, Special Human Development Report 1999", New York: UNDP

Shaw, Timothy M., Sandra MacLean & Maria Nzomo (2000), *Going Beyond States and Markets to Civil Societies in Thomas C. Lawton, James N Rosenau and Amy C. Verdun (eds) Strange Power: Sharing the Parameters of International Relations and International Political Economy*" (Aldershot, Ashgate.

Shaw, Timothy M. (1999) "Forward: Global/Local States, Companies and Civil Societies at the end of the Twentieth Century" in Kendall Stiles (ed), *Global Institutions and Local Empowerment,* London, Macmillan.

Solita, Collas-Monsod (1998) in Vivienne Wee (ed), *Trade Liberalisation: Challenges and Opportunities for Women in Southeast Asia and Beyond.*

SPEED (2001), "Report of a market survey of the dairy industry in Kenya and Rwanda: Prospects for developing Ugandan Dairy Industry and increasing on Exports.

Treadaway, Julian (1974), *Uganda: Studies in Development.*

Twinamatsiko, N. (2001), "Dairy Production: The Role & Economic Importance of Dairying" in Joseph Mukubi (ed) *Agriculture in Uganda Vol.I V: Livestock & Fisheries (NARO),* Kampala, Fountain Publishers.

Twinamatsiko N. (2002), "The Informal Milk Market in Uganda, in Proceedings of the Regional Workshop on Milk Marketing: From Producers to Consumers: Processes for Policy, Legal and Institutional Change in Milk Marketing," sponsored by RELMA, Whitesands Hotel, Mombasa November 25-28.Tybout & Westbrook (1995).

UNBS (2000), "Uganda Standard: Code of Hygienic Practice for Milk & Milk Products", (Kampala).

UNCTAD/ICC (2001), "An Investment Guide to Uganda; Opportunities and Conditions," March, (New York and Geneva, United Nations)

UNDP (1999), "Human Development Report 1999," New York, Oxford University Press.

UNDP "Uganda Human Development Report," Kampala (Various issues).

Wilson J.S & V.O. Abiola (eds) (2003), *Standards and Global Trade: A Voice for Africa*. Washington, DC: World Bank.

World Trade Organization [WTO] (2002) "Trade Data" (Geneva) (http: //www.wto.org) (Accessed December 2002).

Yanikkaya, Halit (2003), "Trade Openness and Economic Growth: A cross-country empirical investigation" in *Journal of Development Economics*, Vol 72, No.1 October, Elsiever, New York.

Magazines

The Economist Magazine, 13 – 19 May 2000.
Newsweek Magazine, 29 April 1990.

Newspapers

The New Vision, 15 June 2000.
The New Vision, 10 August 2000.
The New Vision, 22 June 2001.
The New Vision, 4 August 2000.
The New Vision, 21 July 2001.
The New Vision, 22 July 2001.
The New Vision, 22 June 2001.

Notes

[1] The Bahima had been driven away from this area by a cattle disease, which killed almost all their animals and the invasion of tsetse flies from northern Tanzania in the 1920s. (Young & Lowery, 1977).

[2] Dr Musinguzi (2002). 'Conflicts and Community Conservation in Lake Mburo National Park'. Post Graduate Dissertation, MUST (unpublished).

[3] Dr Babiha hailed from Toro in western Uganda.

[4] Interview Dr Berinda, with the District National Agricultural Advisory Services (NAADS) Coordinator, Mbarara district, March 2003).

[5] The government set such low prices for coffee for instance, that farmers rarely could meet their costs of production and this forced many to cut down their coffee plantations in favour of matooke cultivation, particularly in Ankole. (Kasfir, N: 1994).

[6] Interview with Dr Berinda: NAADS Coordinator Mbarara district, May 2003.

[7] Bushenyi district has always had the highest concentration of dairy farmers for exotic cattle in the region and country as a whole, even up to day, as will be illustrated in chapter five, largely because of the conducive climatic conditions.

[8] Interview with Mr Mukaira in Bushenyi, March 2003

[9] It should be noted here that people in Bushenyi have always been more dynamic and developmental than their counterparts in other parts of Ankole, arguably because they have had higher literacy levels due to the larger number of high schools and technical schools in the district. Also, people from Bushenyi have been noted in Uganda's history as always receptive to change and ready to adopt to new ideas and this could explain why these dairy farmers were innovative and able to survive during the hard times.

[10] Zero grazing refers to feeding cattle in a stable or confined place without taking them out to graze in the field.

[11] Annual export amounts of dairy products have not exceeded $500,000 for the last five years (Uganda Bureau of Statistics, 2000). Average annual imports of dairy products like powdered milk, cheese, UHT milk varieties and butter particularly from South Africa, however, are significantly higher at $2.3 million, indicating that there is an important domestic market for milk and milk products that has not yet been fully exploited.

[12] Flush season refers to that period of the year when milk production is very high. It is usually the wet season and farm gate prices for milk tend to plummet.

[13] Mugisha Odrek Rwabogo (2002 Edition): Uganda's Districts Information Handbook: Fountain Publishers, Kampala.

[14] 2002 Uganda Population and Housing Census: Uganda Bureau of Statistics, Nov. 2002.

[15] It is worth noting here that the distribution of rainfall in the Ankole milk shed area varies rather considerably between the districts of Bushenyi and Mbarara and Ntungamo. Milk yields in the dry season are about half of those in the wet season and this results in the scarcity of milk which pushes up the farm gate prices. There is often surplus milk during the rainy season. Some of this surplus milk is just wasted or churned into local butter, which is distributed freely in some areas, to neighbours or sold cheaply to local communities. This is because the available market cannot buy all the milk produced. The availability of natural pastures and water influence dairy production to a considerable extent. This was particularly highlighted by the recent 1999 drought in the region.

[16] Interview with Mr Mukaira at his home in Bushenyi, June 2003.

[17] Interview with Dr Berinde, NAADS Coordinator, Mbarara District, March 2003.

[18] The dairy sector currently contributes about 20 per cent to the food processing industry. The food industry in-turn contributes about 4.3 per cent to the national GDP. Though small, this contribution is steadily increasing. www.ugandainvest.com/ Dairy.PDF

[19] In the past, farmers used and expected to receive government support in the form of agricultural inputs and subsidies. With liberalisation, however, all these have disappeared forcing farmers to fend for themselves.

[20] A milk shed area refers to that area producing the larger amounts of milk in a country or region.

[21] The prices in some parts of Ankole at times go as low as Ug sh 50 during the wet season

[22] Price fluctuations here refers to the unstable and frequent variation in prices offered by the milk vendors and traders.

[23] Interview with Production Coordinator, Mbarara District, May 2003.

[24] The manure collected from zero-grazed cows is used by mixed farmers to grow crops for food and sometimes for sale.

[25] The Rutamwebwa and Kamujobe families acquired cross-breeds before 1988.

[26] Rushere where the interviews were conducted is approximately 96 km from Mbarara town.

[27] Inflamation of teats is easily treated traditionally by smearing the teats with cow-dung mixed with ashes known as *(okuhomera)*.

[28] Many parts of Ankole were noted to have unclean water, and farmers do not know how to purify it. In Nyabushozi particularly, water has a bad stench and looks very dirty, which could arguably be a source of many cattle diseases in the area.

[29] Interview with Quality Control Manager, DDA Jan-May 2003.

[30] Interview with Quality Control Manager, DDA Jan-May 2003.

[31] For instance, the Banyankole Kweterana Growers Co-operative Union, one of Ankole's strong co-operatives, was dismantled during the mid 1990s as a result of the government's decision to privatise parastatals

[32] Interview with Mr Makaaru, Chairman BUDICO, June 2003.

[33] The most common cattle diseases in Ankole include East Coast Fever *(amashuyo)*, tick fever *(engoha)*, anthrax *(koto)*, biliharzia *(emishundo)*, day sickness *(kagarura)*, bruslessis commonly referred to as contagious abortion *(okutoroga)*, as well as trypanosmiasis *(ekipumpuru)*. Many farmers also indicated that mastitis, which is the inflammation of the teats, is also a major cattle disease in this area and hence the services of regular veterinary attention are required.

[34] The withdrawal period is the time taken for the after effects of drugs to be cleared from the milk of a lactating cow.

[35] Interview with the production officer, Bushenyi District, Jan. 2003

[36] Interview with the District production Officer, Mbarara, March 2003.

[37] Also referred to as formal and informal milk chains respectively.

[38] Boundaries between the two chains often shift, for instance, in the dry season, when vendors also try to establish contact with suppliers in an effort to ensure a steady supply.

[39] Interview with the Production Manager, GBK, April 2003.

[40] Interview with Mr Kasheka, a peasant farmer in Bwizibweera, Kashari, 2003.

[41] Both these categories are often referred to as milk hawkers who deal in loose, unprocessed milk.

[42] Interviews with milk traders and vendors in Ankole and Kampala, January – June 2002.

[43] Interview with Quality Control Manager, DDA, April 2003.

[44] Interview with Quality Control Manager, DDA, April 2003.

[45] DCL is currently being privatised and will soon be sold off to private entrepreneurs

[46] Jerrycans were banned by the MAAIF last year but this ban has been ignored by hawkers.

[47] The demand for imported items has squeezed the household milk budget and many health-conscious Ugandans have cut down or completely cut out their daily milk intake.

[48] Farmers in this case deliver the milk themselves.

[49] From the farm level, milk ought to be transported in refrigerated vehicles but in the absence of such, it should be kept at a sustained temperature of below 10^0c before it is processed. When milk comes out of the cow's udder it is at 37^0c (the temp of the body of a cow). If the udder is diseased the milk contains numerous micro-organisms and if the udder is not diseased it will contain very few. But the growing and multiplying of these micro-organisms must be prevented. So processors should/must cool the milk to 4^0c or less. In Ankole, however, due to limited resources, maintaining or cooling the milk temperature at 10^0c can work/is acceptable until it reaches a dairy plant. And before any product is made, pasteurisation has to be done to destroy pathogenic micro-organisms. (Interview with production manager, GBK, May 2003).

[50]It should be mentioned here that, although liberalisation led to increased milk production and also led to increased participation in milk marketing of formal and informal market agents, the milk hawkers seem to have increasingly crippled the milk processing sector. Although initially real farm gate prices increased, the lack of regulation hampered effective redistribution of benefits, hence, the closure of several milk processing plants and the gradual fall in real farm gate prices of milk today.

[51] For detailed information and figures see Bank of Uganda (various years), Quarterly Bulletin of Statistics, Kampala.

[52] The dairy industry in the West for instance, is one of the most highly protected and subsidised industries. Yet in Uganda, when the economy was liberalised, these private investors had to tussle it out alone. For more details and information on Western Dairying see Falvey Lindsay & Chantalakhana Charan (eds) (1999) Small Holder Dairying in the Tropics, ILRI (International Livestock Research Institute), Nairobi, Kenya. (http://www.cgiar.org/ilri/dbtw-wpd/fulldocs/smhdairy/smhdairy.htm) (Accessed March 2001)

[53] Most of the imported milk products were from Kenya and South Africa.

[54] Interview with a cross-section of people in Mbarara and Kampala.

[55] Interview with the Deputy Director, DDA March 2003.

[56] See John Humphrey & Hubert Schmitz (2001). 'Governance in Global Value Chains' in IDS Bulletin: The Value of Value Chains; Spreading the Gains from Globalisation, Vol. 33 No.3, IDS Publications, Sussex.

[57] It was observed during the fieldwork that in most cases at the sub-county level, the only university graduates were the sub-county chiefs, the veterinary doctors and the agricultural officers and the technicalities of designing development plans for the sub-county are often undertaken by these three people.

[58] Interview with Dr. Zimbe, the veterinary doctor for Kenshunga Sub-country, Mbarara District on 14th May 2003.

[59] Interview with the veterinary doctor for Kenshunga Sub-County, Nyabushozi, March 2003.

[60] Interview with Mr. Bahikaine in Isingiro, May 2003.

[61] Interview with Mr. Kabachenga in Kamatarisi, Biharwe, March 2003

[62] To drench literally means giving cattle medicine orally to guard against intestinal worms

[63] Drenching for cross and exotic breed cattle, is done four times a year.

[64] Except for Bushenyi which has the highest concentration of NGOs in Ankole.

[65] One wonders as to whether their ability to get loans now could perhaps be as a result of state patronage considering that the President of Uganda comes from and raises cattle in this area.

[66] Interview with the Moses Nyabila, Marketing Expert, Land O Lakes (U) in July 2003.

[67] Interview with the veterinary officer, Mbarara District, in March 2003.

[68] Interview with the quality control manager, DDA, in June 2003.

[69] According to several farmers and government officials interviewed in Ankole and Nyabushozi during this research, the government provides technicians and some cement for construction of these tanks at very subsidised costs.

[70] These dams were supposed to be constructed in central positions for use by all farmers in a specific locality.

[71] Interview with Dr. Barigye in Mbarara, in June 2003.

[72] A kraal is a traditional enclosure for indigenous cattle, where they spend the night (a kind of night paddock). It is made of wooden poles and interlocking sticks sometimes with natural thorny shrubs also intertwined. It is usually close to the farmer's house.

[73] One sack of cattle cake goes for Ug sh. 90,000/= yet this can be consumed within a week by 50 cattle.

[74] From my interview with the Marketing Expert, Land O' Lakes (U) Moses Nyabila in July 2003, it was noted that although milk is plentiful here, (creating a condition of "artificial surplus"), in other districts, fresh milk is not so readily available especially in the eastern and northern parts of the country.

[75] Withdrawal periods for particular drugs are not observed. (Interview with the veterinary officer, Mbarara district, in March 2003).

[76] It was interesting to note from the farmers that such an occurrence cannot happen during the dry season because demand for milk is very high then.

[77] Interview with Mzee Kabachenga at his home in Kamatarisi – Biharwe, in May 2003.

[78] The phrase "informal milk traders" is used to refer to all traders and vendors who deal in unprocessed milk.

[79] Interview with Mr. Isha in Kampala, May 2003.

[80] Interview with the Manager, Global markets, Standard Chartered Bank (U) Ltd, June 2003.

[81] For detailed information and figures see: Bank of Uganda (various years), Quarterly Bulletin of Statistics, Kampala.

[82] Interview with the Manager took place at the Factory premises on 16th June 2003 in Mbarara.

[83] Processing farms, therefore, had to incur heavy costs to get the right kind of milk to the factory, which increased production costs and made it difficult to break even as they could not sell enough outputs or products.

[84] For more details and information see: Falvey Lindsay & Chantalakhana Charan (eds) (1999) Small Holder Dairying in the Tropics, ILRI (International Livestock Research Institute), Nairobi, Kenya. (http://www.cgiar.org/ilri/dbtw-wpd/fulldocs/smhdiary/smhdiary.htm) (Accessed March 2001)

[85] Most of the imported milk products were from Kenya and South Africa.

[86] The Monitor, 25th June 2003.

[87] Interview with Mr. Mahmood, former operations manager of Ra-Milk Dairies, in February, 2003.

[88] Interview with Mr. Somani; one of the former factory owners, in March 2003.

[89] See: John Humphrey & Hubert Schmitz (2001): 'Governance in Global Value Chains' in IDS Bulletin: The Value of Value Chains; Spreading the Gains from Globalisation, Vol. 33 No.3, IDS Publications, Sussex.

[90] Isha Muzira: Strategy for Quality Improvement in the Uganda Dairy Sector: A Paper presented at the Dairy Export Symposium, organised by Land 'O' Lakes and sponsored by USAID, at Hotel Africana, Kampala, on 18th June 2003.

[91] Because Kampala is the biggest market for Ankole milk

[92] The reasons consumers gave for preferring raw milk to processed milk were mainly it retained its natural flavour more readily available for those with low incomes. Most respondents confessed that if the price was affordable, they would certainly opt for the processed milk. On the other hand, consumers who preferred processed milk were the sophisticated, high and middle class types, who are health conscious. The reasons they gave for purchasing processed milk was because they felt it was hygienic, of good quality, not adulterated and conveniently packed. These, however, are a small proportion of the population and the market for processors remains limited.

[93] The impetus to competition which is a good thing ushered in by liberalisation also paved the way for deception, cheating and exploitation, by manipulative hawkers.

[94] This is because individual farmers alone cannot survive and benefit much from the sale of such a perishable commodity.

[95] See Mbabazi Pamela's detailed PhD thesis (2004) for lessons from Kenya.

[96] However, this needs to be entered into cautiously, avoiding donor funding as sustainability is essential. Kenya launched a school milk-drinking campaign in the early 1980s with donor funding and it almost back fired when the donor money stopped.

[97] Bornstein Ban: Milk Value: "Got Milk" Article 2, http://wwwmilk.com/value/innovator-spring99.html Accessed March 2004

[98] Certification relates to the quality of the products produced, which must conform to international standards.

[99] See Land O' Lakes Inc International Development (2003) Export Handbook

[100] Workshop Report on the Milk Export Symposium organized by Land 'O' Lakes (U) in Kampala, April 2003 at Hotel Africana

[101] Interview with the production manager, GBK, March 2003.

Index

www.ingramcontent.com/pod-product-compliance
Lightning Source LLC
Chambersburg PA
CBHW070405200326
41518CB00011B/2069